THE INVESTOR'S GUIDEBOOK TO

DERIVATIVES

THE INVESTOR'S GUIDEBOOK TO

DERIVATIVES

Demystifying Derivatives
and Their Applications

STUART R. VEALE

Prentice Hall Press

PRENTICE HALL PRESS
Published by the Penguin Group
Penguin Group (USA)
375 Hudson Street, New York, New York 10014, USA

USA | Canada | UK | Ireland | Australia | New Zealand | India | South Africa | China

Penguin Books Ltd., Registered Offices: 80 Strand, London WC2R 0RL, England
For more information about the Penguin Group, visit penguin.com.

Library of Congress Cataloging-in-Publication Data

Veale, Stuart R.
The investor's guidebook to derivatives : demystifying derivatives and their applications / Stuart R.
Veale. —First edition.
pages   cm
Includes index.
ISBN 978-0-7352-0529-1
1. Derivative securities. 2. Investments. I. Title.
HG6024.A3V43   2013
332.64'57—dc23   2013017458

First edition: September 2013

PRINTED IN THE UNITED STATES OF AMERICA

10   9   8   7   6   5   4   3   2   1

This publication is designed to provide accurate and authoritative information in regard to the
subject matter covered. It is sold with the understanding that the publisher is not engaged in
rendering legal, accounting or other professional services. If you require legal advice or
other expert assistance, you should seek the services of a competent professional.

While the author has made every effort to provide accurate telephone numbers,
Internet addresses, and other contact information at the time of publication, neither the publisher
nor the author assumes any responsibility for errors, or for changes that occur after publication.
Further, the publisher does not have any control over and does not assume any
responsibility for author or third-party websites or their content.

Most Prentice Hall Press books are available at special quantity discounts for bulk purchases for sales
promotions, premiums, fund-raising, or educational use. Special books, or book excerpts, can
also be created to fit specific needs. For details, write: Special.Markets@us.penguingroup.com.

This book is dedicated to:

Danielle Lahmani and Thor Heyeck, as well as the 2,000+
members of the research and development department at Bloomberg
Inc. it has been my pleasure to train over the last 8 years.
Your enthusiasm for learning and insightful questions have
made our time together a delight.

The author would like to thank Jeanette Shaw and her staff at
Prentice Hall Press for all their efforts in turning out this book.
Any remaining errors are the author's responsibility.

CONTENTS

FOREWORD

I finished the second edition of my book on investing called *Stocks Bonds, Options, Futures* (*SBOF*) in 2001. While the second edition was still selling well, it was also overdue for an update. Over the last 12 years, much has changed in the way stocks and bonds were priced, traded, analyzed, packaged, and marketed. Specialists on the NYSE were replaced with designated market makers. The volume of trades executed on the dark pools soared. Derivatives on rainfall and wind had become hot products. Twenty-four-hour trading became a reality. The variety of exotic options exploded. Exchange-traded funds became the fastest-growing financial product in history.

I started out to write the third edition of *SBOF*, but it quickly became clear the industry had become too broad and too complex to comfortably fit in one text. Therefore, after discussing it with my publisher and readers, I decided to break the book into four manageable volumes:

- *The Investor's Guidebook to Derivatives*
- *The Investor's Guidebook to Alternative Investments*
- *The Investor's Guidebook to Fixed Income Investments*
- *The Investor's Guidebook to Equities*

My hope is that by expanding the book into four volumes, I'll be able to make them more comprehensive, include more examples, and make the books more useful to my readers.

While I made every effort to proof the text, there will undoubtedly be errors for which I assume full responsibility. It is my intent to update these volumes frequently and, therefore, I welcome my readers' suggestions on which topics should be added, expanded, and omitted in future editions. Please email your questions, critiques, and comments to stu@invest-perform.com. I hope to answer every email I receive.

This book was prepared from sources believed to be reliable but which are not guaranteed. The research analyst(s) who is primarily responsible for this research and whose name is listed on the front cover certifies that: (1) all of the views expressed in this research accurately reflect his or her personal views about any and all of the subject securities or issuers; and (2) no part of any of the research analyst's compensation was, is, or will be directly or indirectly related to the specific recommendations or views expressed by the research analyst in this research. Opinions and estimates constitute our judgment as of the date of this material and are subject to change without notice. Past performance is not indicative of future results. This material is not intended as an offer or solicitation for the purchase or sale of any financial instrument. Securities, financial instruments, or strategies mentioned herein may not be suitable for all investors. The opinions and recommendations herein do not take into account individual client circumstances, objectives, or needs and are not intended as recommendations of particular securities, financial instruments or strategies to particular clients. Each reader must make independent decisions regarding any securities or financial instruments mentioned herein.

INTRODUCTION

Few topics are as controversial today as derivative instruments. To some, derivatives are simple tools that allow market participants to efficiently and effectively manage their risks. To others, derivatives are weapons that allow market participants to thwart regulations, exceed risk limits, hide market exposures, and threaten the very fabric of the world's economic system. As with any tool, the answer as to whether the tool is good or bad is determined by the way it is used and who is using it.

A highly trained and skilled teppanyaki chef can wield a razor-sharp knife with blazing speed and thinly slice enough steak for a table of eight in just 30 seconds. A thief can use that same knife to kill and rob a stranger in an alley. The knife itself is neither good nor evil. The same is true of derivatives. If the person using them is a business owner who wants to reduce the risk in a portfolio of stocks in order to increase the odds that his employees will enjoy a comfortable retirement, that's a good thing. A flow trader at a major bank could use that same derivative to hide risk in an offshore account in direct violation of his firm's rules, his boss's instructions, and his jurisdiction's securities laws. It's the intent of the person using it that determines whether a derivative is a tool for good or evil.

This book attempts to demystify derivative instruments and to illustrate how they can be used for both good and evil. This book can be used as a classic text by starting at the beginning and working through it to the end. Each chapter assumes the reader knows the material in the prior chapters. This book can also be used as a reference tool, allowing readers to get a quick description about the creation, pricing, trading, and applications of a particular derivative instrument with which they might be unfamiliar.

Enjoy!

CHAPTER ONE

Derivatives Defined

Derivatives are contracts that derive their value from the value of some underlying instrument or index. They are powerful financial tools that allow individuals, corporations, institutions, and governments to manage and reduce various risks in their businesses and portfolios. In this age of modern finance, global trade, and high volatility of FX rates, interest rates, and asset prices—they are essential tools. While any tool can be used improperly, any suggestion that derivatives are only "weapons of mass destruction" or beneficial only to Wall Street insiders is both absurd and irresponsible.

For example, suppose a US investor buys some 6% 10-year IBM Eurobonds. By doing so, the US investor is taking three primary risks:

Interest rate risk—The investor is betting that euro interest rates will decline, which will cause the bond's market value to appreciate.

Credit risk—The investor is betting that IBM's credit quality will improve, which will cause the bond's market value to appreciate.

Currency risk—The investor is betting that the euro will get stronger against the US dollar, which will increase the return in dollar terms.

If the investor didn't have all three expectations, this would be the wrong investment.

As time goes on, however, one or more of the investor's expectations may change. Suppose, for example, the investor's outlook concerning the euro/dollar exchange rate changes. If so, the investor can:

Sell the investment and replace it—In this case, the investor can sell the IBM bond denominated in euros and replace it with an IBM bond denominated in dollars. This alternative will require transaction charges and perhaps have adverse tax consequences.

Do nothing—The investor hopes that the projected gain from the other two bets exceeds the loss on the euro. It seems a little silly to hold an investment that competes against itself.

Use a cross currency swap to hedge the FX risk—This option eliminates the one bet but allows the others to remain. If the investor's outlook on the euro should revert back to the original, the cross currency swap can be eliminated so that the investor again has the original three bets.

Following the same logic, the investor can use:

- An interest rate swap to eliminate the interest rate risk
- A credit default swap to eliminate the credit risk

Each of these hedges can be "put on" when the investor believes the odds are against them and "lifted" when the investor believes the odds are again with them. As a risk is hedged, it can no longer hurt the investor but also can no longer reward the investor. By buying the bond and hedging all three risks, the investor makes the bond risk free. Of course, since the bond is now risk free, it will only offer the risk-free return—minus the transaction charges for the derivatives, which may be substantial. The bottom line is that these derivatives allow an investor to manage the portfolio of risks inherent in this investment.

Going one step further, options on the derivative contracts not only allow the investor to hedge the risks, but to reverse them without selling the original investment, as depicted in Figure 1.1.

FIGURE 1.1

Hedging the Three Risks of a Eurobond

Risk	IBM Eurobond	Add Swap	Add Option on Swap
Interest risk	Yes	None	Reverse
FX (euro) risk	Yes	None	Reverse
Credit risk	Yes	None	Reverse

Derivatives offer their users power and flexibility. This book examines all of the major types of derivative instruments with an emphasis on how they can be used to solve practical problems.

CHAPTER TWO

Forward Contracts

In a forward contract, the terms of a transaction are all agreed to today—but the actual exchange for the underlying instrument doesn't occur until sometime in the future. The underlying instrument can be a single stock, portfolio of stocks, a single bond, a portfolio of bonds, a stock or bond index, an interest rate, a commodity, a currency, an economic indicator, or an environmental statistic (rainfall, average temperature).

More precisely, a forward contract is a private contract between two parties in which one party agrees to buy—and another party agrees to sell—a certain quantity of a certain underlying instrument with certain characteristics at a certain price with certain performance guarantees with delivery to occur at a certain time and location and with disputes settled in a certain way in a certain jurisdiction.

Obviously, the key word is *certain*. Like all contracts, the parties want a contract that deals with every possible contingency so there is no ambiguity. For example, suppose two parties agree to a transaction for a vintage 1965 Mustang (all original with 40K miles).

The parties agree on a price of $50,000, but the buyer asks for 30 days to put the money together. The seller agrees provided he can continue to use the car until it is to be delivered in 30 days. The two parties shake hands and go their separate ways agreeing to execute the physical exchange of car for cash in 30 days.

Unfortunately, this deal has many remaining ambiguities that may come back to haunt the parties. For example, suppose:

- The seller, in a state of seller's remorse, decides that before he delivers the car he wants to take it on a long road trip. In fact, he takes the car on a trip around the perimeter of America. In doing so, he doubles the mileage on the car. The buyer might be outraged. However, since the buyer asked for the extra 30 days to pay, and since no maximum number of additional miles during the extra 30 days was specified, legally the buyer may be stuck.

- One day before delivery the seller takes the car for a last (short) trip. The right rear tire shreds—doesn't just go flat—but completely shreds. The seller calls a flatbed tow truck and has the car towed to his tire dealer. Once there, the seller gets the bad news that he can't buy just one tire because doing so would throw the car out of alignment. So he puts four new tires on the car at the cost of $1,000. On delivery day, he demands payment of $51,000 instead of $50,000—arguing that the buyer will be the beneficiary of the new tires and therefore the buyer should pay for them. The buyer argues that the car can't be delivered without tires and that by continuing to drive the car the seller assumed the "tire risk." The seller says, "Well, if that's how you feel, I'll go get four mismatched bald tires and put them on the car." The deal goes downhill from there!

- One day before the car is due to be delivered, the car is stolen and the seller cannot deliver it. In this case, does the seller owe the buyer a penalty payment for failing to adequately protect the car prior to delivery—or does the theft cancel the contract due to *force majeure*? Most contracts have a *force majeure* clause, which makes the contract unenforceable in the event of an act beyond control of the parties. The debate then becomes, was this theft preventable?

There are some steps that everyone who uses forwards can take to reduce contract ambiguity. First, try to think of and address every possible contingency in the contract itself. This is why a contract for a seemingly simple transaction can be quite long. This is also why working with a very experienced dealer and experienced legal counsel to draft the agreement is essential. The contract should be drafted under the laws of a state with a large body of case law—such as Delaware or New York. By doing so, if a dispute arises, there will be precedents that will guide both parties toward a quick resolution. The parties should also consider including an arbitration clause so that any disputes can be resolved quickly and inexpensively.

Forward contracts are used by hedgers to reduce their risk and/ or speculators who want to try to make a profit. Let's start with an example using two hedgers.

Suppose Company A mines iron ore. The company has teams of geologists that fly around the world seeking out large concentrated deposits of iron ore. Once a large deposit is located, the company negotiates with the land owner for extraction rights, builds the necessary infrastructure (roads, bridges, railroad tracks, and the like) to extract the ore, and then sells the extracted ore. As an ore producer, the company is most profitable when the price of iron ore is high. Company B is a steel company. Company A's product is one of Company B's raw materials. Since Company B's customers are only willing to pay but so much for steel, Company B is happiest when the price of iron ore is low.

Suppose the spot price (price for immediate delivery) of iron ore typically fluctuates between $120 and $240 a ton. At $240 a ton, Company A makes a fortune—but Company B loses money. At $120 a ton, Company B makes a fortune—but Company A loses money.

To reduce their respective risks the companies enter into a forward agreement in which Company A agrees to sell and Company B agrees to buy 1,000 tons of iron each month for the next year. Regardless of the then current spot price, both parties agree that the monthly exchanges will be at $180 a ton. At this price, both companies can make a profit, but neither will make a killing—and neither will suffer a huge loss.

Of course, depending upon what happens to the spot price of iron ore during the agreement, one company will be unhappy it entered into this contract. If, over the term of the contract, the spot price of iron ore averages over $180, Company A will regret the decision. If the price of iron ore averages under $180, Company B will regret the decision. Thus, while this forward contract allowed both companies to lock in a price, only after the contract ends will they know which company benefitted from the contract.

As another example of contracts using hedgers, in the US, farmers often sell their crops before they even plant them. In the late winter/early spring, farmers look at the forward prices for the following fall for their crops and work backward to see on which crop, if any, they can make a profit. Suppose a farmer has 100 acres that are suitable for growing either corn or soybeans.

If the farmer grows corn, the farm will product 200 bushels an acre for 20,000 bushels, which can be sold forward at $6 a bushel for $120,000 in gross income. Subtracting an estimated $3 a bushel in expenses leaves the farmer with a projected return of $60,000 net.

If the farmer grows soybeans, the farm will produce 50 bushels an acre for 5,000 bushels, which can be sold forward at $15 a bushel = $75,000 gross income. Subtracting an estimated $2 a bushel in expenses leaves the farmer with a projected return of $65,000 net.

Thus, soybeans is the more lucrative crop. If neither crop offers an adequate return, the farmer will take the year off and allow the fields to go fallow. Instead of growing a crop, the farmer will work on repairing fences and barns, rebuilding machinery, and so forth.

By locking in a price for the crop, the farmer eliminates the risk that in the fall the spot price will be so low that the farmer takes a loss. Of course, the farmer also eliminates the possibility of making a greater profit if the spot price in the fall is higher. On the other side of this transaction is Kellogg's, Con Agra, or another user of the crop that wants protection against the price being too high.

As a final example, let's look at two speculators. Suppose the 1 year forward price of gold is $2,000. One speculator believes that a year from now the price will be much higher and, therefore, agrees to buy 100 ounces at $2,000 in a year. The buyer is said to "go long." Anyone with a long position wants the value to rise. Another speculator believes the price of gold in a year will be much lower and agrees to sell the first speculator the 100 ounces of gold at $2,000 in 1 year. The second speculator has the short side—he or she hopes for a price decline. If in a year, the price of gold is:

- $1,500, then the short side will buy 100 ounces in the spot market at $1,500 each, deliver it to the long at $2,000, and have a $50,000 ($500 times 100 ounces) profit. The long has an equal-size loss. (The seller can also deliver 100 ounces from its portfolio. Economically, the result is the same.)

- $2,800, then the short side will have to buy 100 ounces in the spot market at $2,800, deliver it to the first speculator at $2,000, and have an $80,000 ($800 times 100 ounces) loss. The long has an equal-size gain.

Forward contracts are a "net sum zero loss game," meaning that the winner wins the same amount the loser loses—but since both parties have transaction charges (legal fees, dealer charges, overhead) the net win is always smaller than the net loss. They are also completely voluntary. Both sides have to believe the contract benefits them, or they wouldn't sign it.

CHAPTER THREE

Forecast Price vs. Forward Price

Suppose that the spot (current) price of a 1 troy ounce of gold is currently $2,000. Now, further suppose that 1,000 people at random were asked the following question: "What do you think the spot price of gold will be 1 year from today?" It wouldn't be surprising to get answers ranging anywhere from $500 to $5,000. Any of the 1,000 answers could be correct because the only way to answer a question that is phrased this way is with a guess. The guess can be an educated guess—or a number just selected at random. The 1,000 answers have to be guesses because no one knows (and no one can know) what the actual spot price of gold will be in a year. The reason the spot price of gold in a year can't be known is that at anytime in history there are simply too many unknown variables that will impact the price of gold. While the variables change, as of this writing the major uncertainties include:

- Argentina's and Venezuela's meltdown
- The Middle East Spring

- Iran's and North Korea's quest for nuclear weapon capabilities
- China's desire to replace its paper reserves with hard commodities
- The euro's potential demise
- The US Fed's relentless quantitative easing
- Unexpected changes in mining production

Likewise, because of the way the following questions are phrased, the only way they can be answered is with a guess:

- What will Apple stock sell for in a year?
- What will the US dollar/euro exchange rate be in 3 months?
- What will the 10-year US Treasury yield be in 8 months?
- What will a bushel of corn cost next fall?

When questions are phrased like the ones above, they are asking for a forecast—a fancy name for *guess*. While the guess can be educated, it is always still just a guess.

Determining the Forward Price

Now, however, suppose two parties are going to enter into a forward contract where one party will deliver to the other 100 ounces of gold in 1 year. What is the fair price for the parties to put into the forward contract they will sign today for an exchange of dollars for gold that won't occur for a year? Neither party knows what the value of gold will be in a year nor can either party accurately forecast the price. Given this uncertainty, how can the parties agree on a "fair price" to put in their contract?

The only way the short (seller) can enter into this contract and not take an extreme price risk is to:

1. Buy the gold today—at today's spot price.
2. Store the gold for a year—and incur all the expenses required to safely store it.
3. Price the gold in the forward contract at today's spot rate plus storage costs.

For example, suppose the following:

FIGURE 3.1
Calculation of Forward Price

Expenses (per ounce)	
Today's spot price	$2,000
Transaction charge to buy gold	$20
Secure transportation of gold to/from vault	$30
Rental of secure storage space	$20
Insurance against fake gold—other loss	$20
Cost of money[1]	$170
Fees received from lending gold to short sellers[2]	–$10
TOTAL	$2,250

1. The seller can either borrow the money necessary to buy the gold and incur interest expense for which it will have to be reimbursed—or the seller can take money out of interest-bearing instruments, losing the opportunity to earn interest. Thus, whether the seller incurs an interest expense or an opportunity cost, there is a "cost of money."

2. Since lending gold will generate fees for the seller, it reduces the cost of storing gold.

In this case, the seller could buy the gold today in the spot market at $2,000, pay the net $250 to carry the gold in inventory—the so-called cost of carry—or simply the "carry," and agree to sell the gold in a year for $2,250 and by doing so, eliminate any price risk. Thus, the forward price is simply the spot price plus the cost of carrying the gold in inventory. If the forward price doesn't equal the spot price plus the cost of carry, the possibility would exist for investors to make a risk-free arbitrage profit.

Suppose the above costs all stayed the same but the forward price was $2,300. If this forward price existed, investors would:

- Upon execution of the contract, sell gold for delivery in a year for $2,300.
- As soon as they signed contracts to sell the gold in a year, they would buy it in the spot market for $2,000.
- Over the next year, they would absorb the $250 costs of carrying gold in inventory.
- Upon delivering the gold at $2,300 in a year, they would make a risk-free $50 profit.

Of course, if everyone:

- Sold gold for delivery 1 year from now, then the 1-year forward price would decline.
- Bought gold today, the spot price would rise.

The arbitrage would only stop when the market returned to equilibrium—meaning that the Spot Price + Carry = Forward Price.

Note two important things about pricing. First, an investor's forecast is irrelevant when calculating the forward price. All of the forecasts and expectations of the world's innumerable buyers and sellers are captured in the spot price. The forward price just adds the cost of carry to the consensus spot price. The fact that the forward price is higher than the spot price does *not* mean the market thinks the price of gold is going up. It only means that it costs money to store gold. Between December 1980 and December 1982, the price of gold fell from above $800 to below $400, and yet on every day the forward price was higher because it always costs money to store gold.

Since the forward price is equal to the spot plus the cost of carry, a change in either the spot price or the cost of carry will cause the forward price of gold to change.

- Changes in the spot price normally result in nearly equal changes in the forward price.
- Changes in the cost of carry are normally the result of changes in the cost of financing.
- If interest rates go up, it costs more to finance the storage of gold.

If this is all there is to forward pricing, how does this become a multibillion-dollar business for dealers? Suppose a relatively small jewelry manufacturer uses 100 ounces of gold per month, and the owner wants to hedge the business against a possible rise in the cost of gold over the next 5 years.

- The manufacturer could hedge the risk by buying all the gold it will need for the next 5 years (100 ounces × 60 months = 6,000 ounces). This would require the outlay or borrowing of $12,000,000 to purchase the metal and also require incurring the associated costs of storage.
- The manufacturer could enter into a series of forward contracts with a major dealer in which the dealer agrees to deliver 100 ounces of gold to the manufacturer each month.

The second approach is almost always preferable. First, the company may not have the necessary capital or credit to buy and store 5 years' worth of gold. Second, the manufacturer may not want the hassle of arranging for the purchase, storage, and transportation of gold. Third, and most compelling, the dealer may be able to sell the manufacturer's gold at a lower price than the jewelry firm's forward price—and yet still make a profit. This last reason is the key to the entire industry. Consider the information in Figure 3.2.

FIGURE 3.2

Differentials in the Cost of Carry

Expenses (per ounce)	Manufacturer	Dealer
Today's spot price	$2,000	$2,000
Transaction charge to buy gold	$20	$3
Secure transportation of gold to/from vault	$30	$20
Rental of secure storage space	$20	$10
Insurance against fake gold or other loss	$20	$0
Cost of money	$170	$35
Fees received from lending gold to short sellers	–$10	–$20
TOTAL	$2,250	$2,048

The dealer's costs will be much lower due to its size and scale. If the dealer sells gold to the manufacturer at $2,230 in a year, the manufacturer saves $20 (and the hassle) and the dealer makes $82. The key is for the dealer's cost of carry to be below the customer's.

OTHER UNDERLYING INSTRUMENTS

Since the forward price of most underlying instruments is simply the spot price plus the cost of carry, it is easy to calculate the forward price of other underlying instruments besides gold. For example, suppose XYZ Inc. common stock is currently selling for $100. If the stock pays no dividend, then the limited income the holder earns from lending it to short sellers should cover all the other costs of carry (record keeping, insurance, and the like) with the exception of financing. If the 1-year spot rate is 5% and the stock pays:

- No dividend, then the 1-year forward price would be $105 ($100 Spot + $5 Cost of Carry).
- A $3 dividend, then the cost of carry would decline to $2— making the forward price $102 ($100 Spot + $5 Financing – $3 Dividends).
- A $7 dividend, the forward price would be $98 ($100 Spot + $5 Financing – $7 Dividends). The lower forward price does not suggest that the market thinks the price will fall. It only means that a holder makes money ($2) when storing this stock.

As another example, suppose XYZ bonds are paying 8%, the short-term borrowing rate for 1 year is 3%, and the bonds are selling in the secondary market at $900. In this case, the 6-month forward price would be:

Spot + Cost of Borrowing – Bond Income
$900 + ($900 × 3% × .5) – ($1,000 × 8% × .5) = $900 + $13.5 – $40 = $873.50

If the underlying instrument is an agricultural commodity, there are two additional factors that need to be considered when calculating the forward price. The first is that some agricultural commodities have a slippage rate when stored. If a buyer wants 20 tons of corn in 3 months, then the seller will have to buy the corn today, store it, and deliver it to the agreed location in 3 months. Suppose the seller buys the corn, delivers it by railcar to storage silos, then 3 months later, has it reloaded on railcars for final delivery. In each step, some corn will be lost. Loading the railcars will cause some waste. Emptying the railcars into storage silos is not 100% efficient. While the corn is in the silo some percentage will be crushed or lost to vermin. Extracting the corn from the silo to reload it on railcars is also not perfectly efficient. The bottom line is that in order to deliver 20 tons of corn in 3 months, the seller may have to buy 21 tons today as 1 ton is lost along the way.

The second is that the spot price falls each year when the new crop comes in and changes the relationship between supply and demand. As the spot price changes, so does the forward price. How much a new crop depresses the spot price depends on the success of each year's crop. Some crops that are grown in both the Northern and Southern Hemisphere have two times per year when significant new supply is added.

As a last example, money can also be priced forward. The forward rate for money is calculated using the two offsetting spot rates. For example, in order to calculate the 1-year interest rate in a year, the 1-year and 2-year spot rates are used. We know that the future value (FV) of the following two alternatives must be the same in order to eliminate the possibility of arbitrage:

- $1 invested at the 1-year rate and then reinvested at the 1-year rate, 1-year forward
- $1 invested for 2 years at the 2-year rate

If the combination of investing successively at the two 1-year rates resulted in a greater FV than the 2-year rate, then everyone would borrow at the 2-year rate and invest at the two 1-year rates.

This would cause the 2-year rate to rise and the 1-year rates to fall until they were equal. The opposite would occur if the FV of the 2-year rate exceeded the two 1-year rates, as shown in Figure 3.3.

Forward Rate as Offset for Two Spot Rates

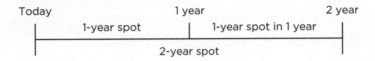

Another way to think about a forward rate is to think like a bank. Consider the following example, which is shown in Figure 3.4 and is based on $1MM notional.

In order to calculate its break-even rate on a 1-year loan in 1 year, a bank would have to buy the money today to lock in its cost and store the money until it is needed—no different than calculating the forward price of gold. In this case, the bank would buy the money (by borrowing it for 2 years) and store it (by investing it for a year).

Example 1: Data for a Forward Rate Calculation

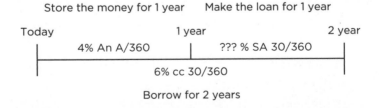

An = Annual

A = Actual

SA = Semiannual

cc = Continuous compounding

The first step to pricing the forward rate is to figure out how much money the bank must invest today in order to have $1MM available in 1 year to lend. We do this, as shown in Figure 3.5, by discounting $1MM for 1 year. Since the 1-year rate compounds annually and the time frame is 1 year, there is no compounding and so the simple interest formula is used to calculate the PV:

$$PV = FV / (1 + (r \times t))$$
$$PV = \$1,000,000 / (1 + (.04 \times 365/360)) = \$961,025.09$$

FIGURE 3.5

Example 1, Step 1: Amount the Bank Needs to Borrow

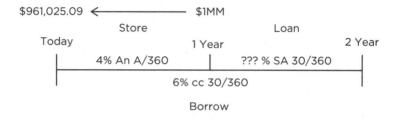

The bank gets the $961,025.09 it needs to invest today by borrowing this sum for 2 years at 6% on a continuously compounded (cc) 30/360 basis, as shown in Figure 3.6. Since it's a cc rate, the calculation has to use the continuous interest formula. The bank, in 2 years, has to pay back:

$$FV = PVe^{rt} = \$961,025.09^{e(.06 \times 720/360)} = \$961,025.09 \times 1.1275$$
$$= \$1,083,552.77$$

FIGURE 3.6

Example 1, Step 2: Amount the Bank Will Pay Back

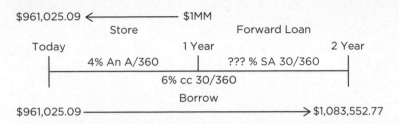

Since this is the amount of money the bank must pay back on its loan, it is also the amount the bank must receive to pay off its loan. The last step is determining the rate the bank must charge on the loan in order to break even. In this case, the $1MM loan must return $1,083,552.77. Since the time frame is a year, but the loan has semiannual payments, the compound interest formula must be used to calculate the break-even loan rate:

$FV = PV(1 + i)^n$

$\$1,083,552.77 = \$1,000,000(1 + i)^2$

$1.08355277 = (1 + i)^2$

$1.04093841 = 1 + i$

$.04093841 = i$ interest rate per period

$i \times 2 = 8.188\%$ annualized interest rate

Naturally, this is only the break-even rate on the cost of funding the loan. The bank would have to add a spread to cover the cost of the credit risk in the transaction, the cost of overhead, a profit, etc. The complete transaction is diagrammed in Figure 3.7.

FIGURE 3.7

Example 1, Step 3: Complete Transaction

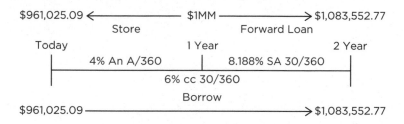

The above calculation can be shortened to the following:

(1-year rate) × (1-year rate in 1 year) = (2-year rate)

$$\left[1 + \left(.04 \times \frac{365}{360}\right)\right]\left[1 + \frac{i}{2}\right]^2 = e^{\left(.06 \times \frac{720}{360}\right)}$$

$$1.040555556\left[1 + \frac{i}{2}\right]^2 = 1.12749685$$

$$\left[1 + \frac{i}{2}\right] = 1.04093841$$

$$\left[1 + \frac{i}{2}\right]^2 = 1.08355277$$

$$i = 8.1888\%$$

As another example, suppose the rates and calendar conventions shown in Figure 3.8 existed and the first year is a leap year.

FIGURE 3.8

Example 2: Forward Rate Calculation in a Leap Year

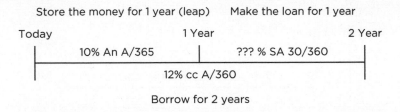

Start by calculating the amount the bank must invest today in order to have $1MM in 1 year, as outlined in the following equations and depicted in Figure 3.9:

$$PV = \frac{FV}{1 + (r \times t)}$$

$$PV = \frac{FV}{1 + \left(.10 \times \frac{366}{360}\right)}$$

[Note: 366 because of leap year]

$$PV = \frac{\$1,000,000}{1.1002740} = \$908,864.54$$

FIGURE 3.9

Example 2, Step 1: Discount the Amount to Be Lent Today

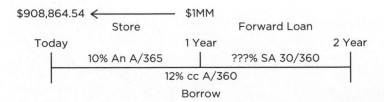

FIGURE 3.10

Example 2, Step 2: The Bank Must Borrow the Same Amount It Must Invest

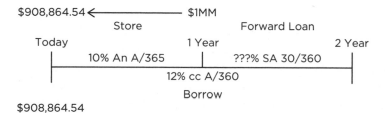

This means that the bank must pay back $1,159,637.49, as described in the following equations and shown in Figure 3.11:

$$FV = PVe^{rt}$$
$$FV = \$908{,}864.54e^{.12(731/360)} \text{ [Note: 731 because of leap year]}$$
$$FV = \$908{,}864.54e^{.24366667}$$
$$FV = \$908{,}864.54 \times 1.27591895$$
$$FV = \$1{,}159{,}637.49$$

FIGURE 3.11

Example 2, Step 3: How Much the Bank Must Have in Order to Pay Off Its Loan

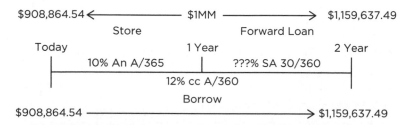

The bank must get the amount it must pay back from the borrower. To earn this sum the bank has to charge 15.37% as derived using the following equations and as shown in Figure 3.12:

$$FV = PV(1 + i)^n$$
$$\$1,159,637.49 = \$1,000,000(1 + i)^2$$
$$\$1.15963749 = (1+ i)^2$$
$$1.07686466 = 1 + i$$
$$i = 7.69\%$$
$$7.69\% \times 2 = 15.37\%$$

FIGURE 3.12

Example 2, Step 4: The Amount the Bank Must Get from the Borrower

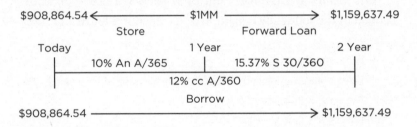

If the 1-year rate rises and the 2-year rate stays the same, the 1-year rate in a year declines.

If the 1-year rate stays the same and the 2-year rate rises, the 1-year rate in a year rises.

FORWARD RATE AGREEMENTS (FRAS)

Borrowers and investors who are worried about interest rates changing can enter into forward rate agreements to manage their risks. Consider the following examples.

A CFO, who expects to borrow $100MM for a year starting in 6 months, looks at the 1-year rate in 6 months and finds out that this forward rate is currently 4.00%. The CFO is worried that, over the next 6 months, the 1-year rate will rise above 4.00% and so wants to lock in the current forward rate while it is available. The CFO would call an FRA broker or a dealer in FRAs and say: "I want to buy a $100MM 6 against 18 at 4.00% on a 30/360."

Translated, this means:

The buyer (the CFO) wants to lock in a 4.00% rate on its future borrowing.

- If, in 6 months, the 1-year spot rate is:
  - Above 4.00%, the buyer will receive the difference.
  - Below 4.00%, the buyer will pay the difference.
- The $100MM is the notional amount.
- The contract rate is the one that starts in 6 months and ends in 18 months.
- The break-even rate is 4.00%.
- Interest is to be calculated on a 30/360 calendar.

If 6 months later, the 1-year rate is above 4.00%, the counterparty pays the CFO the difference between the current 1-year rate and 4.00%. However, if rates decline, and in 6 months the 1-year rate is below 4.00%, the CFO has to pay the counterparty the difference between 4.00% and the current rate.

Suppose that in 6 months the 1-year spot rate 4.65%. In this event, the CFO would receive 65 basis points on $100MM from the FRA. The CFO would pay 4.65% on its loan. The net would be the 4% rate that was locked in by the FRA, as shown in Figure 3.13.

FIGURE 3.13

Calendar for an FRA

Calendar of FRA	
Today	Enter into agreement at 4.00%
In 6 months	1-year rate is 4.65%
In 6 months	Borrow $100MM at 4.65%
In 18 months	Pay $4,650,000 in interest
In 18 months	Receive $650,000 from FRA counterparty
Over term	Net $4,000,000 or 4%

In practice, instead of waiting 18 months to collect the 65 basis points, CFOs normally elect to receive the PV of the 65 basis points on the day the loan is taken out. This eliminates 1 year of counterparty risk and is economically the same as the previous example. Instead of $650,000 in 18 months, the CFO receives $621,118.01 in 6 months. (See Figure 3.14.)

$$\$650,000 / (1 + (.0465 \times 360/360)) = \$621,118.01$$

FIGURE 3.14

FRA Assuming the FRA Is Present Valued

Calendar of FRA	
Today	Enter into agreement at 4.00%
In 6 months	1-year rate is 4.65%
In 6 months	Borrow $100MM at 4.65%
In 6 months	Receive $621,118.01 from counterparty
In 18 months	Pay $4,650,000 in interest
Over term	Net $4,000,000 or 4%

As another example, an investor is worried that when she receives a $50MM inheritance in a year that interest rates will be substantially lower. This reduces the amount of interest she receives from investing her inheritance when she finally receives it. If the current 5-year rate 1-year forward is 6.24%, the investor would tell the dealer, "I want to sell a $50MM 12 against 72 at 6.24% 30/360."

By doing so, the investor locks in a return of 6.24% on her future investment. If in a year, the 5-year spot rate was 5.33%, this FRA would unfold as shown in Figure 3.15.

FIGURE 3.15

Alternative FRA

Calendar of FRA	
Today	Enter into agreement at 6.24%
In 12 months	1-year rate is 5.33%
In 12 months	Invest $50MM at 5.33%
In 12 months	Receive $1,754,773.15 in 1 year from counterparty and reinvest for 5 years at 5.33%[1]
In 60 months	Receive $13,325,000 in interest from investment
Over term	Net $15,600,000 or 6.24%

1. $[50,000,000 \times (.0664 - .0533) \times 5] / [(1 + .0533)^5]$, which can be reinvested.

FX FORWARDS

Exporters who get paid in a foreign currency and importers who are invoiced in a foreign currency are exposed to FX risk. Consider the following example:

A US company exports $2MM of goods to the UK and agrees to accept £1MM in 4 months (122 days) as payment in full when the GBP/USD rate is equal to 2.0000. Before the days of forward contracts, exporters and importers would use back-to-back transactions to hedge FX risk. In this example, to eliminate the FX risk, the company would:

1. Borrow the PV of £1MM from a bank today at the spot rate of 6.00% An A/360.

   £1MM / (1 + (.06 × 122/360)) = £980,071.87

2. Immediately convert the pounds into dollars at today's spot rate. The dollars would be held by the bank as collateral for the pound loan.

   £980,071.87 × 2.0000 = $1,960,143.74

3. Invest the dollars in a bank CD for 4 months at 7% M 30/360.

   $1,960,143.74 × (1 + (.07/12))^4 = $2,006,282.19

In 4 months, when the client pays its £1MM invoice, the US company uses those £1MM to pay off its pound loan. When this loan is paid off, the bank releases the proceeds of the dollar CD to the company. By using back-to-back transactions, the US client can lock in a rate of GBP/USD = 2.0063. Since this rate can be locked in via back-to-back transactions, this must also be the forward GBP/USD rate in 4M. Otherwise, there would be the possibility of arbitrage between the forward rate and the rate that can be locked in via back-to-back transactions.

As another example, consider a US importer who imports televisions with a value of ¥1B from Japan and agrees to pay for them in 90 days. The importer would:

1. Invest the PV of ¥1B today in an instrument that will mature at ¥1B in 90 days. If the 90-day rate is 2.23% An 30/360, the importer needs:

   ¥1B / (1 + (.0223 × 90/360)) = ¥996,934,427 today

2. The investor obtains the yen by purchasing them with dollars at today's spot rate of USD/JPY = 90.

   ¥996,934,427 / 90 = $11,077,049

3. The importer borrows the dollars to buy the yen (or takes them out of an interest-bearing account) so the total cost of the TVs in USD (assuming 4% M 30/360 in US) is:

   $11,077,049 × (1 + (.04/12))^3 = $11,188,189

4. Thus the effective FX rate in 3 months is:

   ¥1B / $11,188,189 = 89.38

Alternatively, the saying "the forward rate equals the spot rate plus the cost of carry" also applies to foreign exchange (FX) transactions. Suppose the spot GBP/USD rate = 2.0000. What is the fair exchange rate to lock in for a transaction that's going to incur in a year? Again, the correct forward rate will be the rate that eliminates the possibility of arbitrage. To determine this rate (Figure 3.16), simply take a pound and:

- Invest it for a year at the rate available in the UK.
- Convert it into US dollars and invest the dollars for a year at the rate available in the US.

- Divide the two future values by each other to determine the forward FX rate.

FIGURE 3.16

Calculating the Future Value of Investing £1.0000 and $2.0000

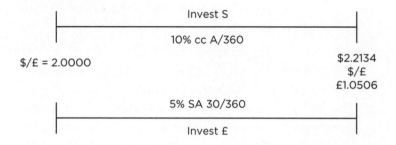

At a forward FX rate of $/£ = 2.1068, the dollar is weaker in the forward market than it is in the spot market. It has to be weaker to offset the higher interest rates available in the US. Again, this does not mean that the market thinks the dollar will weaken against the pound. The higher interest rates in the US in fact suggest just the opposite, as depicted in Figure 3.17. This forward rate is just the rate that eliminates the possibility of a risk-free arbitrage.

FIGURE 3.17

Forward US Dollars Divided by Forward Pounds

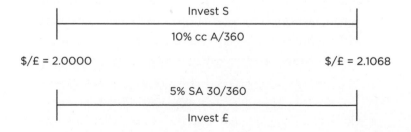

ADVANTAGES AND DISADVANTAGES OF FORWARD CONTRACTS

Forward contracts have numerous advantages and disadvantages relative to other derivative instruments.

ADVANTAGES

Flexible terms—The contracts can be for any size, any start date, any end date, any delivery date, and any delivery location that is mutually agreeable to the two parties.

Customized—The contract can address the specific needs of the parties. For example, instead of just specifying delivery of 100 ounces of gold, the contract can be more specific and specify that delivery be made in the form of 100 1-ounce coins having 99.99% purity. Instead of just specifying delivery of 5,000 bushels of generic #2 corn, a forward contract can specify the color of the kernels, the sugar content, the absence of pesticides and hormones, etc., so that the corn that is delivered is appropriate for an anticipated use, such as canning, popping, or animal feed.

DISADVANTAGES

Counterparty risk—The biggest disadvantage of forward contracts is counterparty risk, the risk that the other party will be either unwilling or unable to honor its commitments. This risk can be managed by diversifying counterparties, performing initial and ongoing comprehensive credit analysis on all counterparties, posting adequate initial collateral, and marking trades to the market when dealing with counterparties with less than pristine credit. For example, suppose you have a contract that allows you to buy gold at $2,000. Each party put up $100 an ounce as initial collateral. As the forward price rises, your counterparty should put up more collateral so that you are protected. If the forward price is $2,400, the collateral should be at least $500 an ounce. With adequate collateralization you are not hurt even if the counterparty fails.

Liquidity—The next disadvantage is liquidity. A forward contract is only as liquid as the other party wants it to be. Chances are, if you want out of the contract, it's because the contract's working against you, which means it's benefitting your counterparty. While any contract can be canceled or amended by mutual consent, obtaining the consent of your counterparty may be very expensive. This risk applies more to contracts between two end-users than to ones between end-users and dealers. One of the ways dealers compete is by offering liquidity on any forward contracts they have with clients.

Reward elimination—Forward contracts always are double-edged swords. They eliminate the risk of an adverse move—but also eliminate the reward of a favorable move.

Price data—Price data is not always readily available. The forward price of a chromium/tungsten 24-inch round bar may not be readily available because all forward transactions are private.

Price discovery—The last disadvantage is price discovery. An investor who calls three dealers to get a price will select whichever dealer offers the best price—but that is no guarantee that is the best price available in the marketplace.

Another dealer may have offered a better price, but an investor can only spend so much time on one transaction. Even if an investor were to call 50 dealers, it would do no good because by the time the investor was finished, the prices of the first 45 would probably have changed.

CHAPTER FOUR

Interest Rate Swaps

An interest rate swap is a derivative contract in which two parties exchange a series of fixed rate interest payments for a series of floating rate interest payments on a specified notional amount. Usually, at the time of the swap, the PVs of both streams of payments are equal. An interest rate swap is the economic equivalent of a series of forward rate agreements linked together.

For example, suppose that today the PV of a 5-year string of annual 8% payments on a 30/360 basis was equal to the PV of a 5-year string of floating rate payments tied to 3-month LIBOR. Two parties could agree to swap 8% for 3-month LIBOR, as shown in Figure 4.1.

FIGURE 4.1

Basic Swap

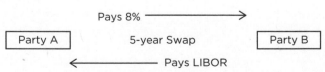

The party paying the fixed rate is known as the fixed rate payer, being long the swap, or being short the bond. The party is paying fixed/receiving LIBOR profits if rates rise—as would someone who was short bonds. The party paying the floating rate is known as the fixed rate receiver, being short the swap, or being long the bond.

The variables with a swap include:

The notional amount—This is the hypothetical amount of principal on which interest will be paid. The notional of swaps ranges from $5MM to multibillions. For most swaps, the notional stays constant over the life of the swap. In a small percentage of swaps, the notional either increases or decreases on a predetermined schedule or based on the performance of an index.

The loan term—Terms run from 6 months to 30 years.

The floating rate—Most swaps utilize 3-month, 6-month, or 1-year LIBOR, although any floating rate that is mutually agreeable can be used, including the rate paid by: T-bills, CDs, commercial paper, and the like.

The payment dates—Most swaps have quarterly or semiannual payments. Usually, the dates that the fixed side pays interest and the floating side pays interest are the same so that the payments can be netted out against each other. However, this is not always the case. Sometimes one side pays more frequently than the other.

The embedded options—Like bonds, swaps can be bullet swaps (no embedded options), callable, or putable.

Pricing Swaps

The value of a swap is equal to the PV of the payments the party receives minus the PV of the payments the party pays. When most swaps are initially created, the PV of the floating payments equals the PV of the fixed payments. Since the difference in PV of the two payment streams is $0, initially a swap has no net value to either party. If party A pays party B $1 and receives $1 from party B, it's a wash. Naturally, if the difference between the present value of the floating payments and the present value of the fixed payments is $200, one party is up $200 while the other is down $200.

The process described next is used to determine the fair fixed rate to swap for LIBOR. Start by determining the PV of the future floating rate payments. Of course, no one can know what the future floating payments will be, so how can they be present valued? While no one knows what the LIBOR rate will be in the future, the forward rate for each period can be calculated from the offsetting spot rates—just like any forward rate. The forward rates can then be used to both determine the floating rate payments that eliminate the possibility of arbitrage and the discount factors for those cash flows. Once the present value of the floating rate side is determined, the one fixed rate that generates payments that have the same PV can be determined. Valuing a 5-year swap with annual payments will illustrate the process:

- Use the 1- to 5-year LIBOR rates to determine the implied forward rates for each annual payment period.
- Use the forward rates to determine the implied floating payments.
- Use the implied forward rates to calculate the discount factors for each payment date.

- Use the forward rates and discount factors to determine the PVs of the forward rates (column 4 × column 5).

As Figure 4.2 demonstrates, the PV of the floating side is 31.1485% of the principal amount.

FIGURE 4.2

Pricing a Swap

Rate	LIBOR AA Rates	1-Year Rate In	Forward Rates	Discount Factor	Present Value
1	4.00%	Spot	4.0000%	.961538	3.8462%
2	6.00%	1 year	8.0385%	.889996	7.1542%
3	7.00%	2 years	9.0284%	.816298	7.3699%
4	7.50%	3 years	9.0141%	.748801	6.7498%
5	7.75%	4 years	8.7558%	.688515	6.0285%
			Sum	4.105149	31.1485%

If the PV of the floating rate side is 31.1485% of principal, the PV of the fixed payments must also be 31.1485%, as shown in Figure 4.3. Thus, the fixed payment X when multiplied by the discount factors, must sum up to equal 31.1485%. In the next equation, the X is factored out:

$$31.1485\% = (X \times .961538) + (X \times .889996) + (X \times .816298)$$
$$+ (X \times .748801) + (X \times .688515)$$
$$31.1485\% = X \times (.961538 + .889996 + .816298 + .748801 + .688515)$$
$$31.1485\% = X \times 4.105149$$
$$X = 7.5875\% \text{ of principal or } \$7,587,500$$

FIGURE 4.3

Projected Payments in Swap

Payment	Floating	Fixed	Projected Payments
1	$4,000,000	$7,587,500	−$3,587,500
2	$8,038,500	$7,587,500	$451,000
3	$9,028,400	$7,587,500	$1,440,900
4	$9,014,100	$7,587,500	$1,426,600
5	$8,755,800	$7,587,500	$1,168,300

Thus, the initial swap rate for a swap with annual payments is 7.5875% vs. 1-year LIBOR. Since initially, the PV of both sides of the swap is the same, both parties value the swap on their books at $0.00.

Immediately after entering into the contract, one or more of the "AA" spot LIBOR rates will change. As the spot rates change, the forward rates also change. This will cause the size of the floating cash flows to change, which, in turn, will cause the discount factors to change.

- On the floating side, the forward rates, the projected cash flows, and the discount rates all change.
- On the fixed side, the discount rates change.

Depending upon whether rates rise or fall, one stream of payments will become more valuable than the other, allowing the swap to acquire a net value. Suppose that immediately after entering into the swap, the FED raises the FED funds rate by 25 basis points and that causes the yield curve to steepen, as shown in Figure 4.4. Figure 4.5 shows the new swap valuation.

FIGURE 4.4

Impact of Rate Changes on Swap

Rate	Old Rates	New Rates	1-Year Rate In	Forward Rates	Floating Payments	Discount Factor	Present Value
1	4.00%	4.00%	Spot	N/A	$4,000,000	.961538	3.85%
2	6.00%	6.30%	1 year	8.65%	$8,650,865	.884980	7.66%
3	7.00%	7.35%	2 years	9.48%	$9,481,217	.808340	7.66%
4	7.50%	7.90%	3 years	9.57%	$9,566,965	.737758	7.06%
5	7.75%	8.25%	4 years	9.66%	$9,661,390	.672760	6.50%
					Sum	**4.065377**	**32.72%**

FIGURE 4.5

Swap Revaluation After Rate Change

Payment	Floating	PV	Fixed	PV
1	$4,000,000	$3,846,154	$7,587,500	$7,295,673
2	$8,650,865	$7,655,843	$7,587,500	$6,714,786
3	$9,481,217	$7,664,043	$7,587,500	$6,133,277
4	$9,566,965	$7,058,110	$7,587,500	$5,597,743
5	$9,661,390	$6,499,801	$7,587,500	$5,104,570
		$32,723,952		$30,846,049
Thus, the new value of the swap = $1,877,903				

The party receiving floating has a swap worth +$1,877,903; the party receiving fixed has a swap worth −$1,877,903.

APPLICATIONS FOR INTEREST RATE SWAPS

The first application most people think of for interest rate swaps (IRS) is changing the interest rate risk of an existing investment or loan. An investor who was receiving interest from a floating rate note (FRN) is exposed to the risk that interest rates will decline. If the investor expected rates to decline, the investor could either:

- Sell the FRN and reinvest in a fixed rate note.
- Enter into an IRS.

In the swap diagrammed in Figure 4.6, the "L in" and the "L out" cancel each other out regardless of whether L is 1% or 20%. By entering into the swap the investor converts L + 150 into an effective 7.50% fixed rate (6% in the swap and a spread of 150 from the floating rate loan).

FIGURE 4.6

Swap Application: Hedging Floating Rate Loan

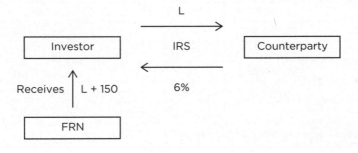

Likewise, an investor who had a fixed rate loan and thought rates would decline could use an IRS to convert an 8% loan to a floating rate loan of L + 200 (600 basis points in + 800 bps out = 200 bps out), as shown in Figure 4.7.

FIGURE 4.7

Swap Application: Hedging Fixed Rate Loan

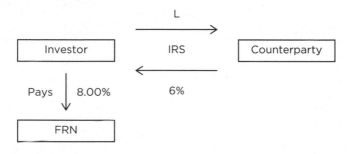

Of course, in addition to hedges, an IRS can also be used by speculators who simply want to bet that rates will rise or fall.

In addition to converting cash flow streams from fixed to floating, a more exotic use of interest rate swaps is to help banks and other organizations manage their yield curve risk. Banks borrow money for the short term and lend for the longer term. Suppose the average term of a bank's borrowings is 1-year and the average term of the bank's loans is 5 years. If the yield curve looks like the one shown with a dotted line in Figure 4.8, the bank can borrow money at 1.00%, lend it at 4.00%, and earn a pre-cost margin of 3.00%. As long as the yield curve retains this positive slope, the bank can roll over its 1-year borrowings as they come due and continue to earn 4.00% on its 5-year loans. Suppose, however, that the yield curve shifts as indicated with a solid line.

FIGURE 4.8
Yield Curve Shift

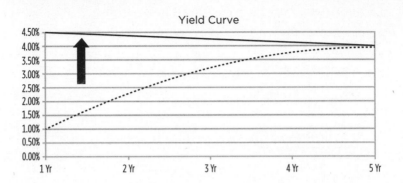

If the yield curve inverts, the bank ends up borrowing at 4.50% to support a loan portfolio that is earning 4.00%. This is not a tenable position over the long term. However, suppose when the yield curve was steep (the 1-year rate was significantly lower than the 5-year rate), the bank entered into the swap shown in Figure 4.9 for 10 years.

FIGURE 4.9
Hedging Yield Curve Shift

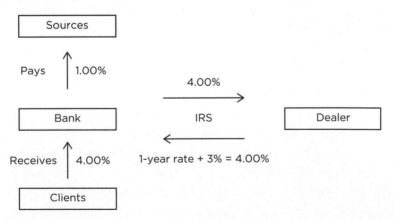

At the start of this swap, the 1-year rate + 3% is equal to 4%, so the PVs of the two sides are equal and the value of the swap is zero. The bank earns a net 3%. Once this swap is established, the bank is protected from the yield curve flattening between the 1- and 5-year points. If the yield curve were to flatten or even invert, as illustrated above, the bank still earns 3% (see Figure 4.10). Of course, if the yield curve were to steepen, the bank would still earn 3%. While this swap eliminates the risk of the yield curve flattening—it also eliminates the profit from a curve steepening.

FIGURE 4.10
After Shift

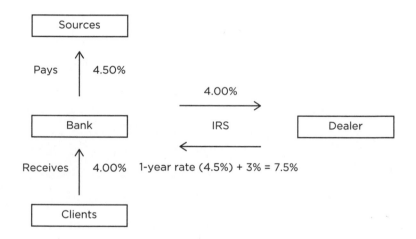

The bank still earns a net 3%.

As another example, suppose a contractor is building a complex over 4 years and needs to draw down $100MM a year for 4 years against a line of credit at a floating rate. When the complex is complete, the contractor will replace the short-term construction financing with a long-term mortgage. The contractor is concerned that rates will rise and wants to enter into a swap to hedge the risk of the construction line. How can a dealer hedge the risk of a loan that has a principal amount that increases at $100MM per year?

The dealer can combine a:

- $100MM 4-year swap that starts immediately
- $100MM 3-year swap that starts in 1 year
- $100MM 2-year swap that starts in 2 years
- $100MM 1-year swap that starts in 3 years

By combining the 4 swaps, the net effect is a swap with an increasing notional value, as shown in Figure 4.11.

FIGURE 4.11
Net Size of Combined Swap

Amount	Years			
	1	2	3	4
$400MM				▓
$300MM			▓	▓
$200MM		▓	▓	▓
$100MM	▓	▓	▓	▓

The three forward swaps (swaps) that start in the future can be priced using offsetting swap rates. For example, the 3-year swap that starts in 1 year can be priced using the offsetting 1- and 4-year swap rates. The LIBOR rates cancel, leaving a familiar forward rate calculation.

FIGURE 4.12

Calculating Forward Swaps

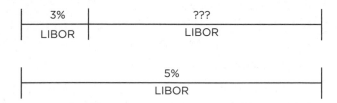

If the rates were quoted quarterly on a 30/360 calendar basis, the forward rate would be:

$$[(1 + (.05/4))^{16}] = [(1(.03/4))^4] \times [(1 + .XXX)^{12}]$$
$$[(1 + .0125)^{16}] = [(1 + .0075)^4] \times [(1 + .XXX)^{12}]$$
$$XXX = .014172 \text{ per quarter or } 5.67\% \text{ expressed annually}$$

As another application, swaps can be used to exploit an arbitrage opportunity. This example will use a floating/floating swap. Suppose the rates shown in Figure 4.13 are the best loan rates that existed in the marketplace. Naturally, the higher the company's credit rating, the lower its borrowing costs. Note, however, that the credit spread between the rates charged the borrowers with higher credit ratings and borrowers with lower credit ratings is not the same in both markets. This may present an opportunity.

FIGURE 4.13

Arbitrage Opportunity

Borrower Rating	Loan Rate Tied to 3-Month LIBOR (L)	Loan Rate Tied to 3-Month T-Bills (TB)
A-	L + 30 bps	TB + 10 bps
BBB-	L + 50 bps	TB + 40 bps
Spread	20 bps	30 bps

Suppose that a company with an A- rating has a business reason for tying its financing to the LIBOR rate. Some possible reasons include:

- The company has an outlook on the LIBOR/T-bill spread and wants to speculate.
- The company holds floating rate assets tied to LIBOR that it wants to match against floating rate liabilities.

Even though the company wants to be tied to LIBOR, its first move should be to borrow with the loan tied to the T-bill rate where its high credit rating saves it 30 basis points. It can then enter into a floating/floating swap with a BBB- company. By doing so, both companies can save 5 basis points. The net result of the swap, as shown in Figure 4.14, is that the:

- A- company borrows at L + 25 net (not L + 30).
- BBB- company borrows at TBs + 35 net (not TBs + 40).

FIGURE 4.14

Arbitrage Opportunity Realized

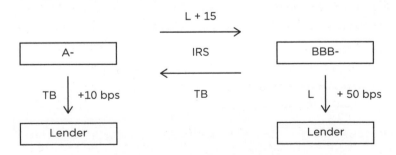

The Role of Dealers in the IRS Market

When swaps were first created, the two parties contracted directly with each other, as illustrated in Figure 4.14. For example, a corporation that was looking to convert a loan from fixed to floating would seek out another company that was looking to convert its fixed rate assets into a floating rate return. The role of the dealer was solely to help seek out the counterparty and provide the requisite documentation. This approach proved to be very inefficient because when a party wanted to do a swap, it had to find a counterparty that not only wanted the opposite exposure—but also wanted it for the same notional amount and for the same term. Finding the right size and term was hard enough. In addition, there were often other requirements a counterparty had to meet in order to be "acceptable." For example, to be acceptable to some companies, a counterparty:

- Had to be from a different industry, so the counterparty wasn't one of the company's competitors. Swaps were off balance sheet and private, so no one wanted its competitors to know its business.
- Had to be politically correct, which often excluded tobacco companies, casino companies, gun manufacturers, liquor companies, and similar entities as potential counterparties.
- Had to have stellar credit ratings—eliminating 95% of the potential counterparties.

To improve the efficiency of the IRS market, dealers started to "make a market." This means that if the fair fixed rate to pay for LIBOR was 4.00%, a dealer might make a market at 4.01% by 3.99%.

Thus, the dealer would pay 3.99% to receive LIBOR, but would demand a customer pay it 4.01% to receive LIBOR, as shown in Figure 4.15. Each client gives up one basis point but in exchange gets an instant execution and gets a counterparty with high credit quality.

In exchange for the 2 basis point spread the dealer earns, the dealer:

- Does the ongoing PV calculations and calculates the net payments the parties will owe or receive on each payment date.
- Assumes the credit risk for both sides; neither counterparty knows or cares about who the dealer has on the other side to hedge its risk.
- Does the record keeping.

In recent years the IRS market has become so liquid and the dealers so competitive that the bid-ask spread is often just a fraction of a basis point.

Dealers try to balance their swap books. Balancing means that both sides have the same notional value with the same terms and same payment dates. By keeping its book balanced, the dealer is hedged against interest rate risk. Figure 4.15 shows the role of dealers in a swap.

FIGURE 4.15

The Role of the Dealer in a Swap

In the event the dealer books more swaps on one side than the other, the dealer will take long or short positions in Treasuries, Treasury futures, and/or eurodollar futures to obtain balance. Suppose a dealer added the swap shown on the right in Figure 4.16, but couldn't immediately find an offsetting swap, how could the dealer hedge its risk?

FIGURE 4.16

Dealer Swap Book Mismatch

Since the dealer is paying floating and receiving fixed, the dealer risk is that LIBOR rises. If LIBOR rises, the dealer will pay out more than it takes in. To hedge this risk, the dealer might take a short position in the 5-year Treasury. If rates rise, the profit on the short position offsets the increase in LIBOR. Obviously, the volatilities of the swap and short position have to be the same. When, and if, the dealer adds an offsetting swap, the dealer can close out the short position in Treasuries.

QUOTING SWAPS

Instead of quoting the price of a swap in percentage terms, dealers instead use a "spread over the equivalent Treasury." Thus, if the dealer priced a 5-year swap at 4.01% by 3.99% and if the 5-year

Treasury yield was 3.50%, the dealer quote would be ".51% vs. .49%." This translates into:

- Clients can lock in payments at a fixed rate of .51% over the current 5-year Treasury for 5 years in exchange for receiving LIBOR.
- The dealer can lock in receipts at a fixed rate of .49% over the current 5-year Treasury for 5 years in exchange for paying LIBOR.

By quoting the spread this way, quotes can last longer—giving clients the opportunity to comparison shop among dealers. Dealers change their spread at a much slower rate than the rate at which the yield on the 5-year Treasury note changes. When a client "hits the bid" or "lifts the offer," both parties look at the current yield of the 5-year Treasury and add the appropriate spread to determine the fixed rate in the swap.

Reselling Swaps

Because the swap market is so liquid, clients can close out their swap positions by simply calling their dealer and canceling the swap. Upon cancellation, the dealer present values both sides of the swap and the party that is behind at this point pays the difference. For example if a client was paying floating and, at termination, the PV of the remaining floating payments was:

- $22,123 less than the present value of the fixed payments, the client would pay the dealer $22,123 to close out the swap.
- $102,333 more than the present value of the floating payments, the dealer would pay the client $102,333 to close out the swap.

In either case, some dealers charge a modest fee (up to $2,500) for early termination to handle the paperwork and cover the cost of rebalancing its swap book.

Advantages and Disadvantages of IRS

Since swaps are just a collection of forward rate agreements, they have the same advantages and disadvantages as forward contracts. On the plus side they are highly flexible. The parties can negotiate:

- Size
- Term
- Payment schedule
- Credit risk management

The biggest drawback of an IRS is the counterparty risk. While the counterparty risk is much lower than the notional value of the swap, it can still be substantial. On a $500MM IRS:

- There is no exchange of principal, thus the counterparty risk is less than $500MM.
- The interest payments are normally "netted out," so the counterparty risk is less than the interest on $500MM.

Instead, the counterparty risk on a $500MM swap is the difference between the PV of the remaining fixed and the PV of the remaining floating rate payments. Since rates can move in either direction, only one party is exposed to the counterparty risk at any time. Since, at the start of the swap, the difference between the two PVs is "0," so is the counterparty risk. As time progresses, the counterparty risk first increases—and then decreases.

- It increases initially because, as time passes, the difference between the fixed and floating can increase, causing the PVs of the future streams to deviate.
- It then decreases because, as time passes, the number of remaining payments declines and so does the PV of both sides of the swap.

Most dealers agree that the greatest counterparty risk occurs near the midpoint of the swap, where rates have had time to change, and yet there are still a substantial number of payments to be made. Dealers can reduce counterparty risk in one or more of the following ways:

- Widening the bid-ask spread for clients with a lower credit quality—the wider spread provides the dealer with compensation for assuming the higher counterparty risk.
- Asking clients to post some collateral that can be sold to cover any loss.
- Marking to the market; as the PV changes, the dealer requires the client to pay the difference in the PVs of the two cash flow streams if the swap moves against them.
- Adding a clause to the contract that requires early termination if the client's credit quality or credit rating deteriorates below a certain level.

Provided that dealers take the necessary steps to protect themselves against credit risk and balance both sides of their books, their risks are both minimal and manageable.

CHAPTER FIVE

FX Swaps

Closely related to interest rate swaps are FX swaps. In a foreign exchange swap, a series of payments in one currency is exchanged for a series in another, as shown in Figure 5.1. Either series can be fixed or floating. As with an IRS, the PV of the two sides is typically equal at the start of the swap and so, initially, the swap has no net value to either party.

FIGURE 5.1

Basic FX Swap

	Pays $ Series ⟶	
Party A	$100MM 5-year Swap	Party B
	⟵ Pays £ Series	

The primary differences between FX swaps and IR swaps are that with FX swaps:

- The payments are not netted out since they are in different currencies.

- The principal is also exchanged (at least at maturity) because they are in different currencies.
- Since the actual exchanges of money are larger, so is the counterparty risk.

Consider the following example assuming the GBP/USD spot rate = 2.0000. Suppose a US citizen is going to receive £100.00 per year for the next 10 years. The US citizen wants to swap the pound cash flows for a series of equal USD cash flows. The steps, as illustrated in Figure 5.2, would be as follows:

- Calculate the forward exchange rate on each payment date.
- Convert the future pound payments into future dollar payments at the forward rates.
- Calculate the PV of the USD cash flows and sum them.
- Calculate "even-size" US payments with the same PV.

FIGURE 5.2

Cash Flows for FX Swap

	UK Spot	US Spot	Forward £/$	Expected Receipts	Convert Dollars	PV $1,650.94	Smoothed Cash Flows	PV $1,650.94
1	2.00%	5.00%	$2.0588	£100.00	$205.88	$196.08	$231.39	$220.37
2	2.25%	5.30%	$2.1211	£100.00	$212.11	$191.29	$231.39	$208.68
3	2.50%	5.60%	$2.1870	£100.00	$218.70	$185.72	$231.39	$196.49
4	3.00%	5.90%	$2.2349	£100.00	$223.49	$177.70	$231.39	$183.97
5	3.25%	6.20%	$2.3025	£100.00	$230.25	$170.44	$231.39	$171.28
6	3.50%	6.50%	$2.3740	£100.00	$237.40	$162.70	$231.39	$158.58
7	3.75%	6.80%	$2.4497	£100.00	$244.97	$154.57	$231.39	$146.00
8	4.00%	7.10%	$2.5298	£100.00	$252.98	$146.14	$231.39	$133.67
9	4.25%	7.40%	$2.6145	£100.00	$261.45	$137.51	$231.39	$121.70
10	4.50%	7.70%	$2.7041	£100.00	$270.41	$128.79	$231.39	$110.20

FX swaps allow investors to add (or subtract) FX risk to an investment. A US investor who buys a bond issued by a Canadian company can use an FX swap to eliminate the currency risk while retaining the interest rate risk and credit risk.

For this next example, let's start with the basic bond rates in both currencies, as shown in Figure 5.3:

- Use them to calculate the spot rates.
- Use the spot rates to calculate the forward rates.
- Use the forward rates to determine the fair £/$ swap rate on a 5.00% 5-year $20MM euro note.

Assume the current £/$ = 2.0000.

FIGURE 5.3

Calculation of FX Swap Starting with Market Rates

Pound Rates					
1	6.00%				
2	6.25%				
3	6.50%				
4	6.75%				
5	7.00%				
Pound Spot Rates		PV of Future Cash Flows			
1	6.00%				
2	6.26%	$58.96			
3	6.52%	$61.32	$57.57		
4	6.79%	$63.68	$59.78	$55.84	
5	7.07%	$66.04	$62.00	$57.91	$53.82

Dollar Rates					
1	5.00%				
2	4.75%				
3	4.50%				
4	4.25%				
5	4.00%				
Dollar Spot Rates		PV of Future Cash Flows			
1	5.00%				
2	4.72%	$44.81			
3	4.43%	$42.45	$39.86		
4	4.12%	$40.09	$37.64	$35.16	
5	3.80%	$37.74	$35.43	$33.09	$30.75

Time	Dollar FV	Pound FV	FX Rate
0	$2.0000	£1.0000	.5000
1	$2.1000	£1.0600	.5048
2	$2.1933	£1.1291	.5148
3	$2.2775	£1.2087	.5307
4	$2.3503	£1.3007	.5534
5	$2.4102	£1.4075	.5840
Time	$ Cash Flow	£ Forward Cash Flow	£ Even Cash Flows
0	−$20,000,000	−£10,000,000	−£10,000,000
1	$1,000,000	£504,762	£819,561.20
2	$1,000,000	£514,786	£819,561.20
3	$1,000,000	£530,725	£819,561.20
4	$1,000,000	£553,421	£819,561.20
5	$21,000,000	£12,263,044	£10,819,561.20
	IRR	8.1956%	8.1956%

CHAPTER SIX

Total Return Swaps

In a total return swap (abbreviated TRS in the United States, TRORS in Europe), a note/loan owner, usually a bank, transfers the entire risk and reward of the note to another party (usually a hedge fund) in exchange for a defined fixed or floating rate return.

In the example shown in Figure 6.1, a bank that borrows floating dollars and lends fixed rate pounds is exposed to three risks:

- FX risk
- Interest rate risk
- Credit risk

In this example, the credit risk is that the money the bank lent to the UK customer might not be repaid on time or in full. The interest rate risk comes from the fact that the bank is receiving a fixed rate on its loan—but is paying a floating rate on its funding. This exposes it to the risk that US$ LIBOR rates rise. The FX risk comes from the fact that the bank is borrowing US$ and lending UK£. The bank is exposed to the risk that the USD will strengthen.

FIGURE 6.1

FIGURE 6.1

Basic Total Return Swap

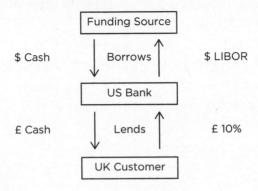

After entering into a TRS with a hedge fund, the bank locks in a 100 bps return by swapping the total return from the loan for US$ LIBOR + 100 bps, which is 100 bps above its cost of funding. This replaces the three risks in the loan with one risk—the counterparty risk of the hedge fund. As shown in Figure 6.2, this is the risk that the hedge fund will be unable to meet its commitment under the terms of the TRS.

FIGURE 6.2

Bank Laying Off Risk with a Hedge Fund

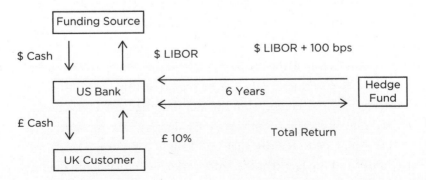

To offset this counterparty risk, the hedge fund usually:

- Puts up a security deposit equal to 10% of the size of the loan to the UK customer in the form of US Treasuries that the bank holds until the swap is terminated.
- Does at least 10 TRS transactions at the same time with the same bank on notes that have different issuers.
- Has the transactions marked to the market.

Requiring the 10% security deposit on each of the transactions ensures that the bank has enough collateral to fully protect itself from counterparty risk on the first loss, even if the recovery is zero. Ideally, the issuers that are swapped by the bank in the 10 TRS have a low correlation, so it is unlikely they will all go bad at the same time. For further protection, when the transactions are marked to the market, the hedge fund puts up more collateral (even if the notes are still paying) in the event that the value of the notes declines due to deterioration risk.

By entering into the transaction with a hedge fund, the bank locks in a 100 basis point spread over its cost of funding. Note that the total return arrow has two heads. If the note generates a positive return, the bank pays the hedge fund the net difference between the total return and $LIBOR + 100. If the return is negative, the hedge fund pays the bank the loss in addition to paying $LIBOR + 100.

The hedge fund hopes that the return from the note consistently exceeds $LIBOR. In this example, the hedge fund benefits if:

- The US dollar weakens against the pound.
- US interest rates decline.
- The credit quality of the loan improves.

If, collectively, these three changes offer a higher reward than risk, the hedge fund will always be the net recipient of the quarterly payment. The hedge fund further benefits from the leverage that a 10% security deposit allows. Figure 6.3 diagrams the swap at inception and in 3 years after US interest rates have declined by 3% and the dollar weakens by 20%.

FIGURE 6.3

TRS Return on Collateral

		Note	Initial	3 Years Later
1	US$ LIBOR Rate		6%	3%
2	GBP/USD		1.0000	1.200
3	Swap Rate		10%	10%
4	Spread	Line 1 – Line 3	4%	7%
5	Security Deposit		$1MM	$1MM
6	Notional on TRS		$10MM	$10MM
7	Notional Times Spread	Line (4 × 6 × 2)	$400K	$840K
8	Interest on Collateral at 3%	Line 5 × 3%	$30K	$30K
9	Return on Collateral	Line (7 + 8) / Line 5	43%	87%

An 87% return on the security deposit (which is raised from investors) leaves plenty of money to offer investors a great return, even after the hedge fund managers take their 2% fee and 20% bonus.

CHAPTER SEVEN

Credit Default Swaps

A credit default swap (CDS) is a derivative contract that provides a way for someone that owns a corporate or municipal note/loan to transfer the credit risk to another party in exchange for paying a fee, as shown in Figure 7.1. The bond/loan owner retains the interest rate risk and FX risk, if any. Note that the premium (a mandatory payment) arrow is shown as a solid line and the protection (a contingent payment) arrow is shown as a dotted line.

FIGURE 7.1

Basic Credit Default Swap

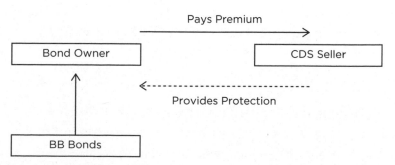

A CDS also allows speculators to take positions on whether the credit quality of a bond or loan will improve or decline. Suppose that the 7% BBB-rated XYZ Inc. 5-year euro note is selling at par ($1,000). An investor, who owns the bond and is worried about the spread widening, could buy 5 years of credit protection at the note's current spread to the interest rate swap curve. Another party, who thought the credit spread would decline, could sell a CDS at the current spread to the curve. If the credit spread widens, the CDS seller pays the buyer the PV of the change. Conversely, if the credit spread narrows, the CDS buyer pays the seller the PV of the change. By convention, today's CDS are marked to the market quarterly on the 20th of March, June, September, and December. They also follow a "100–500 basis point" pricing convention. An example will illustrate.

Suppose it is the 20th of March, a reset date. The current spread of a note to the IRS curve is 180 basis points. The party buying credit protection would pay 180 basis points, and the person selling the protection would receive 180 basis points. This 180 basis point premium is broken into two pieces:

- 100 basis points paid on an ongoing basis
- The 80 basis balance (20 per quarter), which is present valued at the AA swap rate (most dealers have an AA rating), paid up front.

This results in an up-front payment of 353 basis points (assuming quarterly payments and a 5% interest rate swap rate for 5 years).

$$353 \text{ bps} = \frac{20}{(1+.05)^{.25}} + \frac{20}{(1+.05)^{.5}} + \frac{20}{(1+.05)^{.75}} + \frac{20}{(1+.05)^{1}} + \ldots + \frac{20}{(1+.05)^{5}}$$

On the next reset date, if the spread widened by 20 basis points, from 180 to 200, and the discount rate changed from 5.00% to 5.10%, then the PV would change to: 440 basis points.

$$440 \text{ bps} = \frac{25}{(1 + .051)^{.25}} + \frac{25}{(1 + .051)^{.5}} + \frac{25}{(1 + .051)^{.75}} + \frac{25}{(1 + .051)^{1}} + \ldots + \frac{25}{(1 + .051)^{5}}$$

Thus, the protection seller would pay the buyer 87 basis points to compensate the XYZ bond owner for the decline in value due to the decline in credit quality. The seller would have to pay even more, but interest rates rose, so the buyer can reinvest the 87 basis points at a higher rate. A new buyer would pay 440 basis points up front and 100 basis points (25 per quarter) on a continuing basis to buy protection. If the spread is less than 100 bps, then the party selling protection actually receives the initial payment—but still pays the 100 ongoing basis points. If the spread is more than 500 basis points—as is the case with a high-yield bond—the ongoing payment is 500 basis points, and any spread over 500 basis points is paid up front.

SETTLEMENT ALTERNATIVES

When an insured note or loan defaults, the claim must be settled. Over the years, there have been four different methods for settling CDS transactions. Each of these settlement alternatives has advantages and disadvantages. The descriptions that follow merely introduce the various alternatives conceptually. There are numerous details that apply to each one that are beyond the scope of this text.

> **Cash settlement**—The original settlement method was a cash settlement, just like car insurance. When an accident causes the value of a car to decline, the insurance company writes the owner a check to cover the loss. When a default causes the value of a bond to decline, the protection seller writes a check to the bond owner to cover the

loss. Unfortunately, after a bond goes into default, its value in the secondary market can fluctuate wildly ($50 or more during a single trading day) as the estimate of the bond's recovery value changes. This makes it difficult for the bond holder and CDS seller to agree on the size of a mutually satisfactory settlement figure.

Digital settlement—The second settlement alternative was for the parties to agree up front on what the settlement would be in the case of default—typically 60% of face for senior debt and 80% of face for subordinated debt. Of course, this payment could be substantially smaller or larger than the actual loss. While this approach eliminated the disputes between the parties regarding the settlement amount, it created very inaccurate and ineffective hedges.

Physical settlement—The third settlement alternative called for the party who bought the insurance to deliver the bonds to the seller, who then pays par value. This eliminates any disputes over valuation between buyer and seller. The seller then resells the bonds or works through the bankruptcy process in an attempt to recoup as much of its loss as possible. This is not unlike when a car is totaled and the insurance company pays the owner the full value of the car; the insurer then takes the car and sells any undamaged parts to reduce the loss. The problem with this approach is that the volume of CDS contracts can be a multiple of the actual number of notes in existence. A default can create a short squeeze that can cause the bond to trade well above its true value in the secondary market. This reduces the loss payoff to the detriment of the protection sellers.

Auction settlement—The fourth settlement option is auction settlement. In this settlement approach, the dealers who made a market in the CDS submit sealed bids and offers for defaulted notes. The spread between the bid and ask prices the dealers submit in the auction is limited. Once the bids and offers are collected by the auction agent (usually Markit Group Limited), they are sorted with the bid prices ranked from low to high and ask prices ranked from high to low. The resulting sorted list is then divided into three sections:

- One where the bid price exceeds the ask price
- The top half of the remaining bids and offers
- The bottom half of the remaining bids and offers

Where the bid price exceeds the ask price, the ask prices are flipped and trades are executed between the parties. The prices in the third section (lowest bids and highest asks) are discarded.

The prices in the second section (rounded to the nearest eighth) are used to calculate a weighted average price that is used to settle remaining contracts. Consider the example depicted in Figure 7.2.

FIGURE 7.2

Auction Settlement

	Contributions			Sorted	
	Bid	Ask		Bid	Ask
Dealer 1	39.50%	41.00%	Bid > Ask	45.00%	34.00%
Dealer 2	40.00%	42.00%		41.50%	39.50%
Dealer 3	41.00%	43.00%		41.00%	40.00%
Dealer 4	45.00%	47.00%	Top Half	40.00%	41.00%
Dealer 5	32.00%	34.00%		39.50%	42.00%
Dealer 6	38.75%	40.00%		38.75%	42.75%
Dealer 7	38.80%	39.50%	Garbage	38.00%	43.00%
Dealer 8	41.50%	42.75%		32.00%	47.00%

For the top third, the ask prices are flipped and trades are done at the midpoint, as depicted in Figure 7.3.

Orders That Are Crossed

Executable Orders		
Bids	Ask	Trade
45.00%	40.00%	42.50%
41.50%	39.50%	40.50%
41.00%	34.00%	37.50%

Looking at the top pair—a firm that bid 45.0% of face value should be happy to buy at 42.5% of face value. Likewise, a firm that was willing to sell at 40% of face value should be happy to receive 42.5%. The remaining trades that can be settled are done at the weighted average of the best half of bids and offers rounded to the nearest eighth. Figure 7.4 shows the orders used to calculate the settlement price.

Orders Used to Calculate Settlement Price

Best Half	
Bids	Offers
40.00%	41.00%
39.50%	42.00%
38.75%	42.75%

Final price = Weighted average (by size) (40, 41, 39.5, 42, 38.75, 42.75) = 40.667 (rounded to nearest eighth, rounded to 40.625)

The last third of prices represent the lowest bids and highest offers and are simply discarded. Note that this auction process is constantly evolving—for the latest rules and procedures see the Markit.com website.

Applications of CDS

There are numerous applications for credit default swaps:

Hedging existing exposure—The first and most basic application is to hedge existing exposures against credit risk. An investor may want to hedge an existing exposure when the investor becomes concerned about the note's credit quality. When an investor becomes concerned the choice comes down to "selling the note" or "hedging the credit risk." An investor may prefer to hedge the risk if:
- Selling would trigger a tax liability that hedging does not.
- The seller wants to retain the interest rate and FX risk inherent in the note and only wants to transfer the credit risk.
- The note is illiquid and/or the CDS is more liquid.
- The hedged note yields more than selling the note and reinvesting the cash in the money market. For example, if the note yields 7%, the CDS can be purchased at 6%, leaving 1%—when the money market yields .5%, hedging is preferable.

Creating synthetic securities—By buying a 5-year US Treasury and selling credit protection on a company like IBM, an investor creates a synthetic 5-year corporate security. The US Treasury provides the interest rate risk, and the CDS provides the credit risk. Suppose a firm like Consolidated Edison (Con Edison) sells $200MM of new bonds to the market. A portfolio manager is on vacation and misses the offering. The investor can synthetically create additional Con Edison bonds by buying Treasuries and selling credit protection on the bonds. Thus, investors can create unlimited Con Edison notes.

Creating synthetic short positions—By shorting a 5-year US Treasury and buying credit protection on a company like IBM, an investor creates a synthetic short position. The advantages of synthetic short positions over short positions in the underlying notes include the following:

- Investors don't have to borrow the physical bonds and thus reduce overhead.
- Investors don't have to worry about the bonds being recalled at the wrong time.
- It is less likely the position will be outlawed at just the wrong time.

Speculating on the credit quality of a note—Because an investor doesn't need to have an insurable interest, investors can speculate on whether the spread will increase or decrease. The reasons for preferring a CDS instead of the actual notes are the same as those listed earlier for synthetic positions.

Reducing exposure to an issuer or industry—Suppose a fixed income portfolio manager has a 5% exposure limit to an industry and the manager already has 5% invested in airline notes. Oil prices rise and some airline bonds become available at great prices. Because of the allocation limit, the investor must first either sell or buy credit protection on some of the existing bonds in the portfolio to lower the risk to airline credit, before adding new airline bonds to the portfolio.

Timing a default—An investor who expected a company to default in 4 years could purchase credit protection for 5 years and, to offset the cost, sell credit protection for 3 years. If the note goes into default:
- In the first 3 years, the investor both pays and receives, so it's a wash.
- In year 4 and year 5, the investor receives the payoff.
- In year 6 or later, the investor misses out.

Making synthetic commodity and FX plays—Credit default swaps provide indirect ways for investors to make commodity and FX plays:
- An investor who expected oil prices to rise sharply could sell credit protection on highly leveraged oil companies and buy protection on airlines and trucking companies. An investor with the opposite view on oil would take the opposite positions.
- An investor who expected the US$ to strengthen would sell protection on US importers and buy protection on US exporters. An investor who expected the US$ to weaken would do the opposite.

Leveraging lines of credit—When a bank provides a company with an irrevocable line of credit, the bank has to do all the credit work required to approve the credit—but doesn't make the loan. Instead it stands ready to make the loan when and if requested. In exchange, the bank receives a small fee. Since the bank has already done the credit work, it makes sense for the bank to sell credit protection on the company in order to make a profit on its credit work. For example, if XYZ company has an approved $100MM line of credit, a bank has already decided that XYZ is a good credit risk. The bank could then sell $100MM of credit protection via selling $100MM of CDS. If the line was activated, the bank could buy back the CDS and replace the exposure with a loan.

Sovereign Debt CDS

Credit default swaps on sovereign debt have some special characteristics. CDS on sovereign debt protect against repudiation risk and restructuring risk. Usually, all sovereign debt is *pari passu*. However, past experience has taught investors that the longer the term of the debt, the lower the recovery, and therefore the higher the premium.

CHAPTER EIGHT

Equity and Commodity Swaps

When an investor buys equities or commodities, it uses cash that it either borrows or takes out of an interest-bearing deposit. Thus, the investor's return is the return on the equity/commodity portfolio minus the cost of money (typically LIBOR). Figure 8.1 shows the return in diagram form.

FIGURE 8.1

Return from Equity

In an equity swap or commodity swap, the total return of an equity or commodity portfolio (or position) is swapped for a fixed or floating interest rate (usually LIBOR) and replicates the return process shown in Figure 8.1.

For example, consider the equity swap described in Figure 8.2.

FIGURE 8.2

Equivalent Swap Position

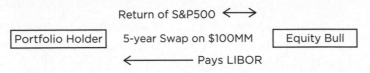

In addition to the notional amount, payment schedule, and term of the swap, the two parties must agree on whether the swap will include or exclude dividends. If the parties agree to include dividends, the swap will be against LIBOR flat. If the swap doesn't include dividends, the payment will be LIBOR minus either:

- An agreed-upon number that offsets expected dividends.
- The actual average dividends.

The parties can be speculators or hedgers. For example, a portfolio holder who owns the S&P 500 and believes the market has peaked can either:

- Sell the portfolio and reinvest the sale proceeds at LIBOR.
- Enter into a swap where the holder pays the return of the portfolio and receives LIBOR.

The choice between these alternatives will be based, in part, on which is cheaper: incurring the sales expenses or paying the spread on the swap. Usually, the swap will be cheaper.

On the other side, the bullish investor would prefer to do the swap instead of actually buying the 500 stocks for one or more of the following reasons:

- The swap allows investors to obtain the return of the S&P 500 without actually incurring the cost of buying 500 stocks and then later selling 500 stocks.

- In some countries, tax stamps and other government charges are incurred when securities are bought and/or sold and can be avoided by doing the swap.
- Finally, in some cases it is illegal for a foreigner to invest in a market; a swap is the only way for the investor to gain exposure to a particular market.

Hedgers would enter into a swap like the one we're discussing if they wanted to postpone capital gains taxes. Suppose that an investor bought $50MM of an Exchange Traded Fund that mirrored the S&P 500 and that 6 months later the shares were up 50%. The investor expects the market to decline, but doesn't want to sell because a sale would trigger capital gains at the short-term tax rates. In some jurisdictions, by entering into a swap, the investor is protected against the downside while prolonging the holding period.

Now, let's take a look at a commodity swap. Suppose an investor who owns aluminum bars (called pigs) and expects the price to decline. The investor could either sell or enter into a commodity swap. In the swap, the holder of the bars would have to receive LIBOR plus the cost of safe storage, as shown in Figure 8.3. Unlike equities, metals incur real expenses such as storage, security, and insurance.

FIGURE 8.3

Aluminum Swap

CHAPTER NINE

Esoteric Swaps

There is also an ever-widening circle of esoteric swaps and unusual derivative structures that are being used to help businesses and governments solve problems and manage risks. For example, consider something as basic as wind. Wind contributes to the profitability of local wind farms and depresses the profitably of airlines.

WEATHER SWAPS

If wind levels in Chicago (aka the Windy City) are high, then local wind farms maximize their production of electricity. However, flights to and from Chicago's O'Hare airport are going to be hours behind schedule. As a result, the airlines are going to suffer significant dollar costs from:

- Canceled flights
- Extra fuel costs

- Overtime costs for pilots, flight staff, and customer service staff
- Meal and hotel vouchers for stranded travelers
- Loss of client loyalty

The two parties can reduce the volatility of their cash flow and earnings by entering into a swap in which the wind farm pays the airlines when the wind level is above normal and the airlines pay the wind farm when wind levels are below normal. By working together, both sides will:

- Have less volatility in their bottom lines
- Be able to have a higher proportion of their capital in debt
- Lower their cost of capital
- Boost the multiple at which their equity trades

If the normal wind is 18 mph, the two parties might agree to a swap with the terms depicted in Figure 9.1.

FIGURE 9.1
Wind Swap

As another weather example, large snowfalls are a liability to many cities because they:

- Cost substantial sums of money for removal—primarily in overtime pay for the sanitation/public works department

- Suppress shopping and entertainment and, therefore, reduce sales and ticket taxes
- Often result in increased police and fire costs

On the other hand, a large snowfall is a huge plus to local ski resorts. More people think of skiing when there is snow on the ground. This not only means selling more lift tickets, but also selling more ski equipment in the resort shops, more meals in the restaurants, and more drinks in the bars. Additionally, ski areas don't have to run expensive-to-operate snowmaking equipment.

Thus, a swap between a city and its surrounding ski resorts could be mutually beneficial. If the typical snowfall level is 40 inches, the two parties might agree to a swap with terms similar to those depicted in Figure 9.2.

FIGURE 9.2

Snow Swap

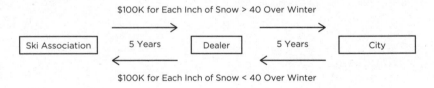

Reinsurance Structured Bonds

As another example, a structured bond deal can take the place of reinsurance. Consider a typical insurance deal where an insurance company insures a $100MM building against loss from fire, earthquake, fire, collision, wind, and other calamities. Traditionally, the insurance company writing the policy would purchase reinsurance from other insurance companies by sharing the annual premium of $4MM with the reinsurance firms.

The primary and reinsurance firms can all share the premium and losses proportionally. Figure 9.3 shows a typical reinsurance structure where each reinsurance company takes 10% of the risk in exchange for 10% of the premium.

FIGURE 9.3

Typical Reinsurance Structure

The reinsurance structure shown in Figure 9.3 can be replicated with esoteric derivatives. The primary insurance company could borrow $60MM from six hedge funds. The primary company would invest $60MM in a high-quality portfolio and supplement the interest with $2.4MM (4% of $60MM) of the premium payment. Thus if the portfolio earned 5%, the bonds would yield 9% (5% + 4%). If there were no claims, the hedge funds would receive 100% of their principal plus 9%, as shown in Figure 9.4. If there are claims, they would eat into the return. A complete loss of the building would probably result in the hedge funds suffering a complete loss.

FIGURE 9.4

Hedge Fund as Reinsurance Company

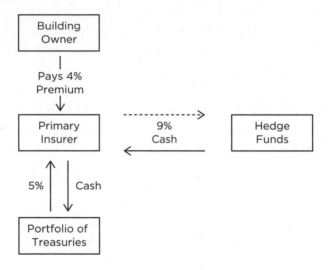

There are advantages of this esoteric structure for both sides:

Primary insurer—For the primary insurer, the chief advantage is that it eliminates counterparty risk in that the primary company has, in a trust account, all the securities it needs to settle claims. The primary company doesn't have to worry about one or more of the reinsurance companies being unable to pay when a large claim is filed.

Hedge fund—For the hedge fund, the advantage is that these types of investments have zero correlation with the stock and bond markets. By adding investments to their portfolio that have low correlations, they improve the return/risk ratio of their portfolios.

TIERED STRUCTURE REINSURANCE

Not all the reinsurance companies must be treated equally; they can be tiered into different groups. Each group becomes responsible for a loss only if the loss exceeds a certain threshold. Look at Figure 9.5. The primary insurer covers all loses by itself up to $20MM. Then, the first tier of reinsurance firms covers the next $20MM. The second tier has the highest absolute risk ($60MM); they only pay if the losses exceed $40MM—in other words, if there is a complete catastrophe.

FIGURE 9.5
Tiered Reinsurance Bonds

Primary Company absorbs first $20MM of losses in a year but takes $2.0MM (50% of premium).

First-Tier Reinsurance Companies A, B, and C absorb the next $20MM for $1.0MM (25% of premium).

Second-Tier Reinsurance Companies D, E, and F absorbs the next $60MM for $1.0MM (25% of premium).

By tiering the risk and reward, different investors can find the risk/reward level (or tranche) that's right for them.

CHAPTER TEN

Futures Contracts

A futures contract accomplishes the same objective as a forward contract—namely, it allows hedgers and speculators to lock in a forward price at the price that eliminates the possibility of arbitrage. Like forward prices, future prices are not forecasts. However, while the objective is the same, the trading and operational mechanisms are much different. Unlike forward contracts, futures contracts trade on an exchange, which give them the opposite advantages and disadvantages of forward contracts. The exchanges incorporate both trading pits and electronic exchanges.

The trading pit is the more traditional trading venue for futures contracts. A trading pit got its name because it is usually a hexagon- to a decagon-shaped pit in the floor with a series of 5 to 10 risers. Each pit hosts the trading for one underlying instrument.

During trading, a futures pit looks like complete chaos. However, just like a beehive or anthill, what initially looks like chaos is actually an orderly and efficient hierarchy designed to accomplish a task. Along the top row are the "floor brokers" of the major dealers. They need to be on the top row to easily receive orders from and pass results to their clerks, who are in the booths surrounding the floor. On the other rungs in the pit are the locals. These are people who bought a seat on the exchange and trade for themselves. They provide liquidity by buying from dealers and selling to dealers when there is no dealer willing to take the other side of a trade. However, they don't work for free. They will try to sell at a price slightly higher than the forward price and will buy at a price slightly lower than the forward price—hoping to make money on the round turns. In this respect, they are like any dealer who tries to earn a return on capital and time.

In the afterhours when the floor is closed or when the floor has been eliminated, a server acts as the exchange and the buyers and sellers trade electronically.

ORDER PROCESS

Suppose two firms want to hedge their risk with regard to the future price of gold.

The gold mine—On one side is a very small gold-mining company that's worried about the price of gold declining below its cost of production. It wants to hedge the price of gold it mines over the next year by locking in a single sale price 1 year from today. For the sake of simplicity, let us assume it expects to produce 100 ounces of gold over the next year.

The jewelry company—On the other side is a small jewelry company that is worried that its cost of raw materials will rise. It wants to hedge the price it will pay for gold so that it can continue to make pieces its customers can afford. It expects to buy about 100 ounces in 1 year.

The obstacles—The firms could enter into a forward contract directly, but both would find it difficult to assess the credit risk of the other. Because the size of the contract is so small, no dealer would want to act as intermediary.

One possible solution is for both firms to open future accounts with brokers that are members of the Chicago Mercantile Exchange (CME), which is where the gold futures contract would trade.

The contract's important specifications are:

Contract Size	100 Troy Ounces
Hours	8:20 a.m. to 1:30 p.m. EST—Open Outcry
Purity	995 Fineness
Position Limit	6,000 contract total / 3,000 delivery month
Settlement	Physical

Before a client is allowed to enter an order to buy or sell, every client is required to post a security deposit with its dealer. Unfortunately, the security deposit is referred to as margin. It is unfortunate because many investors confuse the term "margin" as it applies to the stock and bond markets with "margin" as it applies to the futures markets. Let's look at the difference:

In the cash market—When buying on margin in the stock and bond market, the client puts up part of the purchase price and borrows the balance of the purchase price from a broker. The client pays interest on the borrowed money.

In the futures market—Here, the margin is a security deposit, like a security deposit on an apartment rental. There is no borrowing. At many brokerage firms, large clients actually earn interest on the balance in their margin accounts.

After posting the required margin (usually 5% to 15% of the market value of the positions) and completing the required paperwork, the miner would instruct its broker to sell 1 gold contract that expires in a year. The jewelry company would instruct its broker to buy 1 gold contract that expires in a year. Those orders would be relayed down to the firm's respective floor clerks, who, in turn, would pass the orders to the floor brokers.

- If both orders hit the pit at the same time, the miner's broker will yell out to the entire pit that there was a 1-year contract for sale at the then current forward price—whatever it was. The jewelry company's broker would yell, "Take it!" The two brokers would record the orders as executed with the other broker, and report the trades back to their respective clerks and the exchange. Then, the firms would notify their respective clients that their order was executed and the price at which it was executed.
- If more than one dealer wants to buy the contract that's for sale, the selling broker would simply pick the dealer willing to pay the highest price. If multiple dealers are willing to pay the same price, then the seller would simply select one using any criteria it chose.
- If no dealer wants to buy a 1-year gold contract at the exact moment the seller offers it, the locals will offer to buy the contract—but at a slightly lower price. Because the locals try to buy at a price lower than the true price and sell at a price that is higher than the true forward price, dealers prefer to trade with other dealers whenever possible.

If the spot price of gold is $2,000 and the cost of carry is $100, the fair forward/future price would be $2,100. The forward price and future price must be equal to avoid arbitrage opportunities. The value of the gold contract would be $210,000. In this example, both parties are true hedgers, and hedgers have lower margin requirements than speculators. Thus, both parties only have to meet an initial 5% margin requirement—or $10,500. No money changes hands initially because neither party has yet to benefit financially.

Thus, at the start of the transaction, the two margin account balances would be as depicted in Figure 10.1.

FIGURE 10.1

Margin at Start

	Miner	Price of Gold Future	Jewelry Company
Role	Seller		Buyer
At Inception	$10,500	$2,100	$10,500

At the end of the first day, let's assume the closing price of the future is $2,105. The future price rose by $5 either because the spot price rose by $5 or the cost of carry rose by $5. Regardless of the reason the future price rose, the buyer is ahead by $5 per ounce. At the close of business, the miner's broker takes $500 ($5 per ounce × 100 ounces) from the miner's margin account and sends it to the exchange clearing house. The clearing house, in turn, passes the money to the jewelry company's broker so it can be credited to the buyer's margin account. This process is referred to as "being marked to the market." Thus, at the end of the first day the accounts would read as shown in Figure 10.2.

FIGURE 10.2

Margin at End of Day One

	Miner	Price of Gold Future	Jewelry Company
Role	Seller		Buyer
At Inception	$10,500	$2,100	$10,500
End of Day 1	$10,000	$2,105	$11,000

At the end of each day, the accounts are marked to the market. If a margin balance drops below 50% of its initial level, that market participant must make an additional deposit to its margin account or close out its position. Consider the progression of closing prices listed in Figure 10.3.

FIGURE 10.3

Margin at End of Day 5

	Miner	Price of Gold Future	Jewelry Company
Role	Seller		Buyer
At Inception	$10,500	$2,100	$10,500
End of Day 1	$10,000	$2,105	$11,000
End of Day 2	$9,400	$2,111	$11,600
End of Day 3	$8,400	$2,121	$12,600
End of Day 4	$6,000	$2,145	$15,000
End of Day 5	$10,500	$2,100	$10,500

From day 1 to day 2, the price of the gold future rose by $6, so $600 is transferred from seller to buyer. From day 2 to day 3, the price of the gold future rose by $10, so $1,000 is transferred from seller to buyer. From day 3 to day 4, the price of the gold future rose by $24, so $2,400 is transferred from seller to buyer.

At the end of day 4, the seller is very close to a margin call. The seller could close out the contract by buying back the contract at $2,145. Buying a contract back at $2,145 that was originally sold at $2,100, means a loss of $45 per ounce or $4,500 per contract. Of course, that money has already been removed from the seller's margin account so money would change hands on the way out. Fortunately, the seller decides to hold on for one more day, and gold drops $45 an ounce, taking the margin account back to its original level at the end of day 5.

After a year has gone by, the futures contract reaches its last trading day. Throughout the year, cash has moved back and forth between the margin accounts and the parties have added additional margin when required, as shown in Figure 10.4.

FIGURE 10.4

Margin at End of Year

Role	Miner Seller	Price of Gold Future	Jewelry Company Buyer
At Inception	$10,500	$2,100	$10,500
End of Day 1	$10,000	$2,105	$11,000
End of Day 2	$9,400	$2,111	$11,600
End of Day 3	$8,400	$2,121	$12,600
End of Day 4	$6,000	$2,145	$15,000
End of Day 5	$10,500	$2,100	$10,500
End of Day 361	$13,500	$2,070	$7,500
End of Day 362	$14,500	$2,060	$6,500
End of Day 363	$15,000	$2,065	$6,000
End of Day 364	$14,500	$2,055	$6,500
End of Day 365	$15,500	$2,050	$6,000

Since this is the last day of trading, both parties must either close out their position or go through the delivery process. If they close out their positions as the last trade at $2,050:

- The seller sold at $2,100 and buys back at $2,050—making $50 per ounce, which is already in the seller's account. The mining company then sells its gold in the spot market for $2,050. When the $50 per ounce profit is incorporated into the analysis, the mining company sells for a net $2,100.
- The buyer bought at $2,100 and sells as $2,050—losing $50 per ounce, which has already been taken out of its account. The jewelry company then buys its gold locally. When you add the $50 the jewelry company lost, its total cost is $2,100.

If neither party closes out their positions, then both parties will go through the delivery process. The seller will deliver a 100-ounce bar of gold to an exchange-approved warehouse, and the buyer will show up at an exchange-approved warehouse to buy a 100-ounce bar of gold. In both cases, the parties will pay and receive the then-current spot price for gold. Since delivery occurs at the then-current spot price, both parties can do just as well by closing out their positions during the last trading month and buying or selling their gold locally. For this reason, almost all contracts are simply closed out. Fewer than 1% of contracts actually go through the delivery process.

Note that the delivery process for most futures is not entirely fair. In the case of gold, the seller has the option of delivering a bar as small as 95 ounces or as large as 105 ounces. The seller gets paid for every ounce delivered.

- If the seller has a profit, the seller will deliver a larger bar and will make a per ounce profit on 105 ounces.

- If the seller experiences a loss, the seller will deliver a smaller bar and take a per ounce loss on 95 ounces.
- The buyers receive whatever bars the sellers deliver, and so often must take losses on up to 105 ounces and profits on as little on 95 ounces.

This is referred to as a "delivery option." Since it benefits the seller, the price of the future contact must be adjusted to reflect its value. Thus, the value of the futures contract is equal to:

Spot + Cost of Carry – Value of Delivery Options = Future Price

Because this delivery option impacts the future price, even market participants who never plan to go through the delivery process should be aware of the option and its impact.

Perfecting Futures Hedges

Suppose that it is June, gold's spot price is $2,000, and an investor decides he wants to sell 100,000 ounces of gold, but for tax purposes, he has to wait until March of the following year to sell. The investor has two options to hedge the sale:

Forward contract—Using this option, the investor enters a contract to sell gold at the forward price of $2,100. In this case, the investor incurs $100 per ounce in carry charges, sells the gold for $2,100 per ounce, and nets $2,000.

Future contract—Here, the investor enters a contract to sell gold in March at $2,100. Again, the investor incurs $100 per ounce in carry charges and is marked to the market for the difference between $2,100 and the then current spot price. The loss or gain on the sale is determined by the spot price in March, as shown in Figure 10.5. The future net gain is fixed.

FIGURE 10.5

Future Net Gain Is Fixed

Spot Price in Next March	Gain/Loss Margin Account	Loss Due to Cost of Carry	Gain/Loss on Sale	Net Gain/ Loss
$2,200	–$100	–$100	+$200	$0
$2,100	$0	–$100	+$100	$0
$2,000	+$100	–$100	$0	$0
$1,900	+$200	–$100	–$100	$0
$1,800	+$300	–$100	–$200	$0

REBALANCING FUTURE HEDGES

There is one twist with regard to using futures contracts as hedges—and that's dealing with the "time value of money" issue. In the last example, the sale of the physical gold occurs in March—and therefore the gain or loss from the physical sale also occurs in March. However in the futures hedge, the margin account is impacted daily. Consider the time line depicted in Figure 10.6.

FIGURE 10.6

Impact of Time on Futures Hedge

June   March

9 Months

Sell 1,000 March Contracts   Sell 100,000 Ounces of Gold

Suppose that in June the investor hedges the 100,000-ounce sale in March by selling 1,000 March gold contracts. At first glance, this may seem correct because each contract is for 100 ounces—but it is not a good hedge. If, immediately after selling the 1,000 contracts, the spot price of gold was to increase by $20, the future price would also rise by $20. Because the price of gold has gone up by $20, the investor will receive an additional $2MM from the sale of the physical gold in March. However, the investor's margin account will also be debited by $2MM *today*. By being debited today, the investor loses not only the $2MM, the investor also loses the interest that could be earned on that $2MM over the next 9 months. In other words, the investor loses the future value of $2MM in 9 months.

Because of the time value of money, a $2MM loss today is not offset by a $2MM gain in 9 months. Instead, a $2MM gain in 9 months is offset by a loss today equal to the PV of $2MM. Thus the future hedge needs to be present valued. If an investor is going to sell 100,000 ounces of gold next March, the investor needs the PV of 1,000 gold contracts to hedge the risk today. If the time is 270 days and the rate is 4.00%, the correct number of contracts would be:

$$1{,}000 \,/\, (1 + (.04 \times 270/360)) = 971 \text{ rounded to nearest contract}$$

Thus, the correct hedge is as shown in Figure 10.7.

FIGURE 10.7

Present-Valuing Futures Hedge

If the price of gold falls by $20, the margin account will suffer a gain today of $1,942,000. This money can be invested and will grow to $2MM in 9 months—which will offset the $2MM loss on the sale of physical gold.

As time passes, both the number of days and the discount rate will change, and therefore so will the number of future contracts that will be required to hedge the risk. For example, in 90 days, the remaining time to the sale will drop from 270 to 180 days. If over those 90 days, the discount rate drops to 3%, the number of contracts now required to have a proper hedge will be:

$$1{,}000 / (1 + (.03 \times 180/360)) = 985 \text{ rounded to nearest}$$
contract

The investor must short another 14 contacts (971 + 14 = 985). Over time the number of contracts will rise as the time to expiration gets shorter. On the last before expiration, the number of contracts would be:

$$1{,}000 / (1 + (.03 \times 1/360)) = 1{,}000 \text{ rounded to nearest}$$
contract

Rebalancing should be done daily.

THE EURODOLLAR FUTURE

A eurodollar (ED) is a dollar that is deposited in a major bank outside the legal jurisdiction of the United States. The bank does not have to be in Europe. Thus, a deposit denominated in dollars held in a major bank in Canada, Brazil, Germany, Hong Kong, or England is considered a "eurodollar deposit." The eurodollars futures contract is used by dealers and clients to hedge short- to intermediate-term interest rate dollar exposures, as well as to speculate on short-term interest rate dollar movements and yield curve shifts. It was created in 1981 by the Chicago Mercantile Exchange and is one of the world's most important and liquid futures contracts. It usually trades more than 1.25MM contracts a day for a notional value in excess of:

$$1{,}250{,}000 \text{ contracts} \times \$1{,}000{,}000 \text{ size} =$$
$$\$1{,}250{,}000{,}000{,}000 \text{ PER DAY}$$

In addition to the contracts that expire on the IMM dates, there are also ED contracts that expire on the third Wednesday of the next 3 months, as shown in Figure 10.8. The underlying instrument for this future contract is a hypothetical $1MM 3-month eurodollar deposit. These hypothetical deposits run from one International Money Market (IMM) date to the next. (The IMM dates are the third Wednesday of March, June, September, and December.) The contracts go out 10 years into the future.

FIGURE 10.8

The Eurodollar Futures

IMM Date MAR	IMM Date JUN	IMM Date SEP	IMM Date DEC	IMM Date MAR
MAR Contract	JUN Contract	SEP Contract	DEC Contract	

The yields on these future deposits are forward rates that are determined by the two offsetting spot eurodollar rates. For example, given the data shown in Figure 10.9, the forward rate for the SEP contract would be 7.715%.

FIGURE 10.9

Pricing the ED Futures Contract

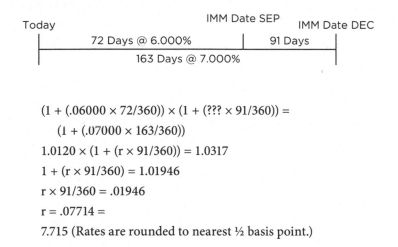

$$(1 + (.06000 \times 72/360)) \times (1 + (??? \times 91/360)) =$$
$$(1 + (.07000 \times 163/360))$$
$$1.0120 \times (1 + (r \times 91/360)) = 1.0317$$
$$1 + (r \times 91/360) = 1.01946$$
$$r \times 91/360 = .01946$$
$$r = .07714 =$$
$$7.715 \text{ (Rates are rounded to nearest ½ basis point.)}$$

The contract is quoted 100.000 − Yield = 92.285. This makes the contract consistent with other fixed-income instruments, that is, the "long" profits when rates decline and the price rises, and the "short" profits when rates rise and the price declines.

If the yield changes by 1 basis point, $25 changes hands between the buyer and seller. Since a basis point is 1% of a percent then:

$1,000,000 is the size of a contract.
$10,000 is 1%.
$100 is 1% of a percent—for a year.
$100 / 4 = $25 is 1% of a percent for 3 months.
A ½ basis point change for 3 months would be $12.50.
A ¼ basis point change for 3 months would be $6.25.

Let's look at a trade between two speculators: one who believes interest rates will decline over the next 72 days (i.e., goes long the contract) and one who believes threats will rise (i.e., goes short the contract). Figure 10.10 shows the interaction.

FIGURE 10.10
Marking ED Position to the Market

	Short	Price of Sept Future	Long
At Inception	$10,000	92.285	$10,000
End of Day 1	$ 9,950	92.305	$10,050
End of Day 2	$ 9,750	92.385	$10,250
End of Day 3	$ 9,575	92.455	$10,425
End of Day 4	$ 9,450	92.505	$10,550
End of Day 5	$ 9,475	92.495	$10,525
End of Day 68	$ 9,825	92.395	$10,175
End of Day 69	$10,150	92.305	$9,850
End of Day 70	$10,400	92.205	$9,600
End of Day 71	$10,525	91.155	$9,475
End of Day 72	$10,650	91.105	$9,350

On the last day of trading, the forward rate becomes a spot rate and the final price/yield is fixed. Instead of using the rate paid by one bank to fix the final price, the exchange surveys many banks and, after discarding the highest and lowest rates, averages the others. All contracts not already closed out are "cash settled," meaning that they are marked to the market one last time at the end of the last trading day. There is no delivery because:

- You can't deliver a eurodollar deposit in the United States.
- The CME can't force a bank either inside or outside the United States to accept a deposit.

Hedging a Future Borrowing

Today is July 3, and a CFO forecasts that her company will need to borrow $500MM for 3 months starting in September in order to meet a short-term cash flow imbalance. The CFO is worried that rates will rise before September, increasing the company's borrowing expense. Once the company borrows its money at a fixed rate in September for 3 months, subsequent rate increases don't impact the company's borrowing expense, so its risk to rates rising starts today and ends in September.

To hedge this risk, on February 10, the CFO should go short the PV of 500 SEP contracts—i.e., 485 contracts. Figure 10.11 shows the calculations used to determine the required number of ED contracts.

FIGURE 10.11

Calculating the Required Number of ED Contracts

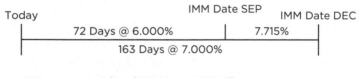

$$500 \text{ contracts} / (1 + (.07000 \times 163/360)) = 485 \text{ contracts}$$

Note that establishing a valid hedge requires going short the PV of 500 contacts—not 500 contracts. This raises three questions:

1. **Why is it necessary to PV the number of contracts?** The number of contracts must be present valued since the timing of the higher/lower interest payment on the actual loan is different than when the margin account used to hedge is marked to the market. If the CFO shorted 500 contracts, and

the next day rates fall by 10 basis points, the company would *immediately* lose $2MM in its margin account—but will also pay $2MM less in interest in December. If the company loses $2MM immediately, it not only loses the $2MM, but also loses the interest it could have earned on the $2MM. In effect, from today's perspective, the company loses the FV of $2MM. A $2MM loss today does not have the same value as a $2MM gain months in the future.

2. **What date is used for present valuing the number of contracts?** The number of contacts should be present valued from the day the company actually pays a higher or lower interest payment—the IMM date in December. Note that even though the risk ends in September when the company actually borrows the money for 3 months at the then current spot rate, the company actually pays the higher/lower interest in December. If the margin account has a profit in September, that profit can be reinvested until the IMM date in December. In December, the gain in the margin account plus the interest it earns should offset the higher interest payment. Likewise, if in September the margin account has a loss, that loss has to be financed until December, when it is offset by the interest savings stemming from investing at a lower rate.

3. **What discount rate is used in the calculation?** The correct rate is the spot rate to the date the company pay interest. In this example, it's the DEC spot rate.

Based on the calculation depicted in Figure 10.11, the CFO would go short 485 SEP ED contracts today. Let's assume that on the next day the SEP forward rate popped up by 10 basis points. In this case, the company's margin account would be credited with:

485 contracts × 10 basis points × $25 per basis point =
$121,250

Since the cost of borrowing rose by 10 basis points, the company will have to pay $500MM × .0010 × .25 = $125,000 in December. The $121,250 that is credited to the company's margin account tonight can be invested for 162 days and should grow to $125,000 in December—offsetting the company's higher interest expense. As with the gold future, this hedge needs to be rebalanced because the passage of time and the change in the discount rate will alter the number of futures contracts necessary to hedge the risk.

Hedging a Future Investment

Today is July 3, and a CFO forecasts that, in September, her company will have $700MM to invest for 6 months. The risk is that rates will decline before September. How this 6-month risk is hedged will depend upon the nature of the 6-month investment the company plans to make.

If the company plans to invest where there is a single interest payment at the end of 6 months, then ideally the CFO would hedge it with a 6-month ED contract. Of course, there is no 6-month ED contract—but, fortunately there doesn't have to be. By buying or selling two successive 3-month contracts, investors and hedgers can create a synthetic 6-month contract, as shown in Figure 10.12. After all, the 6-month rate must equal the two 3-month rates compounded, otherwise it creates an arbitrage possibility.

FIGURE 10.12

Creating a Synthetic 6M ED Future

IMM Date SEP		IMM Date DEC		IMM Date MAR
	SEP Contract		DEC Contract	
	Synthetic 6M Contact			

So, if the company is going to make a 6-month investment from the IMM date in September to the IMM date in March, the company needs to hedge its exposure as a single 6-month risk. To hedge that risk, the company would link the SEP and DEC contracts together and treat them as one contract. Today, the CFO would go long the PV of 700 SEP and the PV of 700 DEC contracts. In September, the risk ends and therefore the hedge also should end. The SEP contracts expire, so they end of their own accord. The DEC contracts have to be sold, as shown in Figure 10.13. The gain/loss in the margin account should offset the loss/gain on the actual investment.

FIGURE 10.13

Managing the ED Hedge with 6-Month Payments

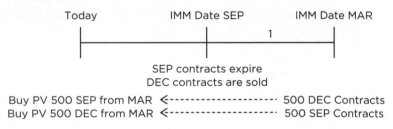

By linking contracts, synthetic securities as long as 10 years can be created.

If the company plans on making two successive 3-month investments, then it needs to hedge each 3-month period as a separate risk, as shown in Figure 10.14.

FIGURE 10.14

Managing the ED Hedge with 6-Month Payments

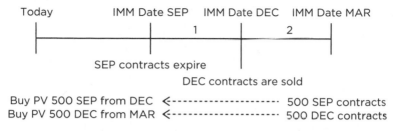

Yield Curve Plays

Let's assume a speculator expects the yield curve to quickly steepen between the 6-month point and the 18-month point. The investor could go long a 6-month note and short an 18-month note. Alternatively, a speculator could go long a 6-month ED strip and short an 18-month ED strip. Using ED strips instead of cash instruments might provide greater liquidity. To balance the position so it has no net exposure to a parallel shift, the investor must have an equal exposure to both the long and short side. Note that the short and long positions in each contract can be netted out against each other. (See columns 2, 3, and 4 in Figure 10.15.)

FIGURE 10.15

Using ED Futures to Hedge Yield Curve Risk

Contract	Long	Short	Net	Initial
0–3M	3	1	2	97.000
3M–6M	3	1	2	96.250
6M–9M		1	1	95.750
9M–12M		1	1	95.450
12M–15M		1	1	95.000
15M–18M		1	1	94.750

In the event of a parallel shift in the curve, the result would be no gain or loss, as shown in Figure 10.16.

FIGURE 10.16

Result of a Parallel Curve Shift

Contract	Long	Short	Net	Initial	Current	Profit/Loss
0–3M	3	1	2	97.000	98.000	$200
3M–6M	3	1	2	96.000	97.000	$200
6M–9M		1	1	95.250	96.250	–$100
9M–12M		1	1	94.750	95.750	–$100
12M–15M		1	1	94.500	95.500	–$100
15M–18M		1	1	94.450	95.450	–$100
					Sum	"0"

However, if the yield curve were to steepen (Figure 10.17 and Figure 10.18), the speculator would make money on both the long and short positions. Flattening (Figure 10.19 and Figure 10.20) would cause both sides to be losers.

FIGURE 10.17

Result of a Steepening

Contract	Long	Short	Net	Initial	Current	Profit/Loss
0–3M	3	1	2	97.000	97.900	90
3M–6M	3	1	2	96.250	97.000	75
6M–9M		1	1	95.750	95.750	0
9M–12M		1	1	95.450	95.100	35
12M–15M		1	1	95.000	94.300	70
15M–18M		1	1	94.750	93.900	85
					Sum	355
355 ticks × $25 per tick = $8,875						

FIGURE 10.18

View of Steepening

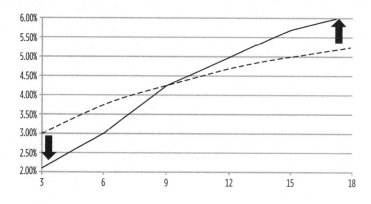

FIGURE 10.19

Result If Curve Flattens

Contract	Long	Short	Net	Initial	Current	Profit/Loss
0–3M	3	1	2	97.000	96.100	−90
3M–6M	3	1	2	96.250	96.000	−75
6M–9M		1	1	95.750	95.900	−15
9M–12M		1	1	95.450	95.800	−35
12M–15M		1	1	95.000	95.700	−70
15M–18M		1	1	94.750	95.600	−85
					Sum	−370
				−370 ticks × $25 per tick = $9,250		

Pricing an ED Swap as the Equivalent of an Interest Rate Swap

FIGURE 10.20

Comparison of ED Strip

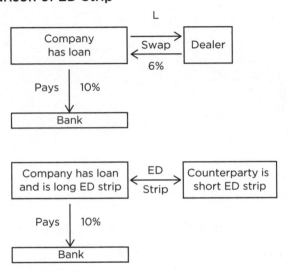

In both cases, the 10% the company pays the bank is converted into a floating rate. As rates fall, the following occur:

- The PV of the swap, which starts at 0%, benefits the company as rates decline and it receives a net payment.
- In the ED strip, the company benefits as rates decline, since the value of the strip rises and so do the credits to the company's margin account.

Since both alternatives allow the company to convert fixed rate financing to floating, the two alternatives can be arbitraged against each other. Since they can be arbitraged, the rates must be the same.

Otherwise, companies would always use the more attractive of the two alternatives to hedge and this would push prices toward equilibrium. Consider the pricing example shown in Figure 10.21 and Figure 10.22, where:

Column 1: Number of the Time Periods

Column 2: Name of the ED Contract for the Period

Column 3: Start Date

Column 4: End Date

Column 5: Actual Day Count in Period

Column 6: Price of the Future's Contract

Column 7: Interest Rate Implied by the Futures Contract

Column 8: Value of the Convexity Option (see below)

Column 9: Equivalent Futures Rate

Column 10: Implied Floating Payment (Notional × Col 9 × Col 5 / 360)

Column 11: Discount Factor

Column 12: PV Floating Payment (Col 10 × Col 11)

Column 13: Date Count 30/360 Basis (not shown)

Column 14: Fixed Rate Payments Assuming Quarterly Payments (not shown)

Column 15: The PV of the Fixed Payments (not shown)

Column 16: The Process Repeated for Semiannual Payments (not shown)

Column 18: The Process Repeated for Annual Payments (not shown)

Column 20: The Process Repeated for a Single Semiannual Payment (not shown)

FIGURE 10.21

First Half of Swap-Pricing Spreadsheet

		Period Start Date	Period End Date	Actual Day Count	ED Future Price	Equiv. Future Rate	Convex Adjust (bps)	Implied Forward Rate	Implied Floating Payments	A/360 Discount Factor	PV Floating Payments
Notional Amount	$100,000,000									SUM PV	$29,079,516.46
1	Spot	5/18/2006	6/19/2006	32	NA	5.00%	0	5.00%	$444,444.44	0.995575221	$442,477.88
2	June	6/19/2006	9/18/2006	91	94.56	5.44%	0	5.44%	$1,375,111.11	0.982070658	$1,350,456.27
3	Sept	9/18/2006	12/18/2006	91	94.25	5.75%	0	5.75%	$1,453,472.22	0.968001032	$1,406,962.61
4	Dec	12/18/2006	3/19/2007	91	94.03	5.97%	0	5.97%	$1,509,083.33	0.953610259	$1,439,077.35
5	Mar	3/19/2007	6/18/2007	91	93.87	6.13%	0	6.13%	$1,549,527.78	0.939059275	$1,455,098.43
6	June	6/18/2007	9/17/2007	91	93.71	6.29%	1	6.28%	$1,587,444.44	0.924362173	$1,467,373.60
7	Sept	9/17/2007	12/17/2007	91	93.52	6.48%	1	6.47%	$1,635,472.22	0.909465134	$1,487,404.96
8	Dec	12/17/2007	3/17/2008	91	93.37	6.63%	1	6.62%	$1,673,388.89	0.894474487	$1,496,803.67
9	Mar	3/17/2008	6/16/2008	91	93.18	6.82%	1	6.81%	$1,721,416.67	0.879315575	$1,513,668.49
10	June	6/16/2008	9/15/2008	91	92.98	7.02%	1	7.01%	$1,771,972.22	0.863984176	$1,530,955.96
11	Sept	9/15/2008	12/15/2008	91	92.78	7.22%	1	7.21%	$1,822,527.78	0.848498605	$1,546,412.28
12	Dec	12/15/2008	3/16/2009	91	92.61	7.39%	1	7.38%	$1,865,500.00	0.832939072	$1,553,847.84
13	Mar	3/16/2009	6/15/2009	91	92.47	7.53%	2	7.51%	$1,898,361.11	0.817380907	$1,551,684.13
14	June	6/15/2009	9/14/2009	91	92.31	7.69%	2	7.67%	$1,938,805.56	0.801795124	$1,554,524.84
15	Sept	9/14/2009	12/14/2009	91	92.14	7.86%	2	7.84%	$1,981,777.78	0.786175134	$1,558,024.41
16	Dec	12/14/2009	3/15/2010	91	92.02	7.98%	2	7.96%	$2,012,111.11	0.770630238	$1,550,593.66
17	Mar	3/15/2010	6/14/2010	91	91.85	8.15%	2	8.13%	$2,055,083.33	0.755074651	$1,551,741.33
18	June	6/14/2010	9/13/2010	91	91.69	8.31%	3	8.28%	$2,093,000.00	0.739539997	$1,547,857.21
19	Sept	9/13/2010	12/13/2010	91	91.52	8.48%	3	8.45%	$2,135,972.22	0.724020222	$1,546,487.08
20	Dec	12/13/2010	3/14/2011	91	91.44	8.56%	3	8.53%	$2,156,194.44	0.708685835	$1,528,064.46

FIGURE 10.22

Second Half of Swap-Pricing Spreadsheet

	SUM PV	$29,079,516.46	SUM PV	$29,079,516.46	SUM PV	$29,079,516.46	SUM PV	$29,079,516.46
		7.0594%		7.1198%		7.2447%		8.5029%
30/360 Day Count	Fixed Rate Payments	PV Quar. Fixed Payments	Semi Fixed Payments	PV Semi Fixed Payments	Annual Fixed Payments	PV Annual Fixed Payments	Zero Fixed Payment	PV Zero Fixed Payments
31	$607,893.87	$604,220.85						
89	$1,745,243.68	$1,705,119.87	$2,373,257.60	$2,318,239.80				
90	$1,764,853.16	$1,695,051.11						
91	$1,784,462.64	$1,685,005.95	$3,579,663.55	$3,378,541.63	$6,057,369.02	$5,711,407.96		
89	$1,745,243.68	$1,621,255.01						
89	$1,745,243.68	$1,595,389.68	$3,520,332.11	$3,215,700.64				
90	$1,764,853.16	$1,587,700.78						
90	$1,764,853.16	$1,562,886.82	$3,559,886.40	$3,149,418.31	$7,204,445.54	$6,360,877.73		
89	$1,745,243.68	$1,521,998.59						
89	$1,745,243.68	$1,499,181.08	$3,520,332.11	$3,020,358.00				
90	$1,764,853.16	$1,493,385.70						
91	$1,784,462.64	$1,487,517.67	$3,579,663.55	$2,979,747.04	$7,224,569.69	$5,996,171.05		
89	$1,745,243.68	$1,433,963.32						
89	$1,745,243.68	$1,413,691.50	$3,520,332.11	$2,846,933.60				
90	$1,764,853.16	$1,409,426.85						
91	$1,784,462.64	$1,405,063.76	$3,579,663.55	$2,813,468.10	$7,224,569.69	$5,656,969.48		
89	$1,745,243.68	$1,355,555.43						
89	$1,745,243.68	$1,337,425.88	$3,520,332.11	$2,692,343.30				
90	$1,764,853.16	$1,334,405.92						
91	$1,784,462.64	$1,331,270.71	$3,579,663.55	$2,664,766.05	$7,224,569.69	$5,354,090.23	$41,002,986.73	$29,079,516.46

Hedging a Swap Book

Now, consider a swap dealer who starts a new swap book. The dealer always wants its swap book to "balance," meaning that the size, term, and payment frequency of the swaps on both sides are equal. In the swap book depicted in Figure 10.23, the dealer's cash flows are all both paid quarterly on the $500 notional for a term of 5 years.

FIGURE 10.23

Dealer Adds a Swap to Book

Suppose that the swap book is brand new and a dealer adds the swap with CP 1 first swap. The dealer is exposed to the risk that rates will decline. The dealer can hedge this risk by going long a $200MM 5-year ED strip, as shown in Figure 10.24.

FIGURE 10.24

Hedge by Replicating Missing Swap

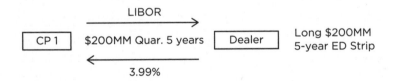

Or suppose a dealer has the swap book shown in Figure 10.25. How could the dealer achieve balance?

FIGURE 10.25

Book "Out of Balance" on Size

In this case, the dealer has a size mismatch. It needs to add $100MM of exposure to the left side to obtain balance. It could go short a $100MM 5-year eurodollar strip to obtain balance.

But suppose a dealer has the swap book depicted in Figure 10.26. How could the dealer achieve balance?

FIGURE 10.26

Book "Out of Balance" on Maturity

In this case, the dealer has no risk for the first 3 years, but in years 4 and 5, there is a $200MM shortfall (see the left side of the above transaction). The dealer needs to go short a $200MM 2-year strip that starts in 3 years—i.e., a $200MM 2-year strip in 3 years.

As dealers add each swap to their swap books, it creates new mismatches in size, term, or frequency that ED positions can balance. Each swap that gets added to the book changes the dealer's net interest rate risk and so requires that the hedge be changed. It is not uncommon for a dealer to buy and sell the same ED contracts several times in the same day to hedge its ever changing interest rate risk.

CONVEXITY OF THE EURODOLLAR CONTRACT

The ED contract, like most futures contracts is not "fair." It has a bias that favors the short side of the trade, as shown in Figure 10.27.

Consider the following example: Suppose the ED contract is priced at 94.00, which equates to a yield of 6.00%. The buyer makes money if the rate goes down; the seller makes money if the rate goes up. The gains in their margin accounts can be reinvested; the losses must be financed. Thus, the short gets to invest when rates are high and borrow when rates are low. The longs have the opposite situation.

FIGURE 10.27

Graph That Explains Convexity of the ED Future

Longs	Yield	Price	Yield	Short
Long Profits and Reinvests Gains at 4.00%	4.00%	96.00	4.00%	Short Loses and Finances Losses at 4.00%
		94.00		
Long Loses and Finances Losses at 8.00%	8.00%	92.00	8.00%	Short Profits and Reinvests Gains at 8.00%

This advantage that the shorts have increases as:

- The time to expiration increases, creating more opportunities to borrow low and invest high
- The volatility of the ED rate increases

To compensate the long for this disadvantage, there is a spread between the forward rate and the rate implied by the futures contract. For example, if the 3-month forward rate starting in 2 years is 5.00%, the future might be priced at 94.98 (5.02%). The extra 2 basis points compensate the long for the convexity effect. Figure 10.28 compares the advantages and disadvantages of the two contracts.

FIGURE 10.28

Comparing Forwards and Futures Contracts

	Forwards	Futures
Advantages	Flexible	Inflexible
	Counterparty Risk	No Credit Risk
Disadvantages	Poor Price Discovery	Excellent Price Discovery
	Uncertain Liquidity	Excellent Liquidity

CHAPTER ELEVEN

Options

With forwards, futures, and swaps, as long as the parties maintain a position, they have absolute obligations to either buy or sell the underlying asset. Options, as the name implies, are different. With option contracts, one party, the buyer, has the right to either enforce the contract—or cancel it. Naturally, it will only enforce the contract if it is to its advantage. Thus, unlike other derivatives, the payoff is asymmetric. Options come in two types: calls and puts.

CALL OPTIONS

A call option contract gives its buyer (the long) the right to buy a certain quantity (contract size) of a certain something (the underlying) at a certain price (strike price) until the contract expires (expiration date). In effect, the owner of a call option has an insurance policy that protects the investor from having to pay a price higher than the strike price until the expiration date. Like any insurance policy, the long buys it by paying a fee (the premium). The fee is paid to the call seller. The seller assumes the role of the insurance company.

For example, an investor buys a 1-year call option on 100 shares of IBM common stock @ $200 per share for $1,000 ($10 per share) from a seller. In 1 year, on expiration day, if IBM is selling for:

- $275—up $75 over the strike
  - The long could exercise the option and force the short to sell 100 shares @ $200. The long can then hold the shares—or resell them in the market for $275, making a profit of:

  $27,500 sale value – $20,000 purchase price – $1,000 cost of option = $6,500
  If it owns them, the short can deliver the long 100 IBM shares from its account.
  If the short doesn't own any IBM common, the short could buy the shares in the market at $275 and deliver them at $200, generating a loss of:
  $20,000 sale value – $27,500 purchase price + $1,000 cost of option = –$6,500

  - The long could instead sell the option for $7,500 [($275 – $200) × 100] – $1,000 cost of option = a $6,500 profit. Likewise, the short could buy back the contract at $7,500, generating a loss of $6,500.
- $205—up $5 over the strike
  - In this case the buyer loses $500, but still exercises or sells to recoup $500 of the initial cost of the option.
  - The long could exercise the option and buy 100 shares from the short @ $200 and either hold the shares—or sell them in the market at $205, making a loss of:

$20,500 sale at market value − $20,000 purchase price − $1,000 cost of options = −$500

- The long could sell the option for $500 ($5 × 100) − $1,000 = −$500
  - $150—down $50 under the strike
    - The long would let the option expire. Why use the option to buy at $200 when the stock can be bought cheaper in the market?
    - The long's loss and seller's gain would be the cost of the option, $1,000.

Note that all of these outcomes exclude transaction charges, which would reduce the returns/exacerbate the losses of the loser.

PUT OPTION

A put option contract gives its buyer (the long) the right to sell a certain quantity (contract size) of a certain something (the underlying) at a certain price (strike price) until the contract expires (expiration date). In effect, the owner of a put option has an insurance policy that protects the investor from having to sell at a price lower than the strike price until the expiration date. Like any insurance policy, the long buys it by paying a fee (the premium). The fee is paid to the short. The short assumes the role of the insurance company.

For example, an investor buys a 6M put option on 5,000 ounces of silver at $40 per ounce for $7,500 (i.e., $1.50 per ounce). In 6M, on expiration day, if silver is selling for:

- $30—$10 under the strike
  - In this case the long makes $42,500.

- The long could exercise the option and force the short to buy 5,000 ounces @ $40. The long can deliver the silver from its own account or can buy it in the market for $30 and then deliver it at $40. The long makes $42,500, and the short, therefore, loses $42,500.

$200,000 sale proceeds – $150,000 purchase price –
   $7,500 cost of option = $42,500

- The long could instead sell the option for $50,000 ($10 × 5,000) – $7,500 cost of option for a profit of $42,500. The short could buy back the contract at $50,000, generating a loss of $7,500 – $50,500 = –$42,500.
- $39—$1 under the strike
  - In this case the long loses $5,000, but still recoups $2,500 of the initial cost of the option.
  - The long could buy 5,000 ounces of silver at $195,000 ($39 × 5,000) and the option to force the short to buy at $200,000 from the option's $200 and either hold the shares—or sell them in the market at $205, making a profit of:

$200,000 sale value – $195,000 purchase price – $7,500
   cost of option = –$2,500

- The long could sell the option for $5,000 ($1 × 5,000) – $7,500 cost of option = –$2,500
- $50—$10 over the strike
  - The long would let the option expire. Why use the option to sell at $40 when the silver can be sold in the open market at $50.
  - The option was an unnecessary insurance policy.

Note that all of these outcomes exclude transaction charges, which would reduce the returns and exacerbate the losses. The four basic option positions offer investors different maximum profit potential, maximum loss, and break-even points, as depicted in Figure 11.1.

FIGURE 11.1

Basic Option Positions and Max Profit, Max Loss, and Break-Even

Position	Max Profit	Break-Even Price	Max Loss
Long Call	Unlimited[1]	K + TC + P[2]	P + TC[3]
Short Call	P − TC[4]	K − TC + P[5]	Unlimited[6]
Long Put	K − P − TC[7]	K − TC − P	P + TC
Short Put	P − T	K + TC − P	K − P + TC

K = Strike Price   P = Premium   TC = Transaction Charges

1. When there is no limit to how high the price of the underlying can rise, there is no limit to how high the price of a call option can go. If there is a limit on the price of the underlying, like when the underlying instrument is a bond, the limit is the price less the strike (at least at expiration).

2. The break-even price is the strike the investor pays plus the two costs (P + TC) that the long needs to recover.

3. The maximum loss is the premium and the TC—assuming the option is worthless at expiration.

4. As the insurance company, the short experiences its greatest profit when the option expires worthless and the short gets to keep the entire premium less any transaction charges.

5. The short can afford to lose the premium minus any transaction charges without taking a net loss.

6. If buying a call can provide the long with unlimited gains, selling the call must expose the short to unlimited losses. That said, it is very rare for a stock price to explode upward. Stocks usually rise slowly and fall quickly. Many traders believe that, in the real world, being short puts is risker than being short calls.

7. Unlike the call, the profit potential from being long a put is not unlimited. This is because the price of the underlying can only go down to zero. Since the long can sell something that is worthless for the strike price, that limits the profits to the strike price minus the premium and transaction charges.

Combining options of various types with various strikes and different expiration dates allows investors to create a smorgasbord of positions. No matter what the investor's outlook, there is an appropriate option position to maximize.

LISTED OPTIONS

Listed options trade on the floor of an exchange, and the exchange clearing corporation is the counterparty for each trade. Two floor brokers, representing the two parties, do the trade so that one party sells exactly the same options that the other party buys. Thus, the exchange's books are always balanced. As soon as the trade is done, the exchange assumes the responsibility of being the counterparty for both parties. Since the exchange takes the credit risk of all trades, the buyers and sellers never have to worry about the actual client behind the broker on the other side of their trade. Eliminating counterparty risk is one of the main benefits of listed options.

As of this writing, there are nine options exchanges in the United States. They are constantly merging to achieve economies of scale.

- BATS Global Markets (BATS)
- Boston Options Exchange (BOX)
- Chicago Board Options Exchange (CBOE)
- CBOE's C2
- International Securities Exchange (ISE)
- NASDAQ Options Market (NOM)
- NASDAQ OMX Philadelphia (PHLX)
- NYSE AMEX
- NYSE ARCA

LIQUIDITY

In addition to eliminating counterparty risk, exchanges also boost liquidity. They do so by standardizing the option contracts so that an investor can buy contracts from one party and later resell them to a different party. The difference between the buy price and sale price is the investor's gain or loss. In this respect, listed options are no different than buying IBM common stock from one party and later selling it to another. Since what is bought is exactly the same as what is sold, once the two trades are completed, the investor no longer has an exposure to IBM.

As part of its standards, the exchange specifies:

- The size of the contract. For example:
  - Each stock option contract is for 100 shares of stock.
  - Each option on futures is for 1 futures contract.
  - Each option on physical silver is for 5,000 ounces.
  - Each option on oil is for 1,000 barrels.
- The spacing between the strike prices depends on the exchange's rules, for example:
  - For stocks below $50, the strikes are $2.50 apart.
  - For stocks between $50 and $100, the strikes are $5 apart.
  - For stocks over $100, the strike prices are $10 apart.
- The expiration dates:
  - Most contracts have a quarterly expiration and use one of the following schedules:
    - MAR JUN SEP DEC
    - APR JUL OCT JAN
    - MAY AUG NOV FEB
  - Many exchanges add contracts, so that one expires for

each of the next 3 months regardless of its longer rotation schedule.

- The trading hours vary from contract to contract.
- The position limits are imposed and limit the number of contracts in which a single party can be long or short in order to keep the markets orderly and prevent someone from taking such a large position they can corner or manipulate the markets.

These standard provisions limit the number of options contracts on a specific underlying instrument. By limiting the alternatives, the liquidity of each contract is improved.

Liquidity is measured four ways:

Percentage of trades that involve the specialists/local traders—The higher the liquidity, the higher the percentage of "customer to customer" transactions. When one customer wants to buy and another customer wants to sell, their two brokers can do business directly. If the fair value of the option is $10, both the buying and selling customer get a price of $10—although both pay their broker's commissions.

Bid-ask spread—As with all markets, the greater the liquidity, the narrower the bid-ask spread. When a customer wants to sell and there is no other customer that wants to buy, the customer's broker will do the trade with a floor specialist or local trader. These professionals provide liquidity—but at a cost. The cost is the bid-ask spread. A floor specialist might agree to buy the option at $9.95 and sell it at $10.05, making $0.10. Spreads for most option contracts are $0.05 although it varies from contract to contract.

Trading volume—Usually, the higher the trading volume, the greater the liquidity.

Open interest—Open interest is the most important measure of liquidity. The open interest is defined by the number of contracts that have been opened, but not yet closed. Suppose that a new 6-month call option on IBM at $240 starts trading, and initially there are four buyers and four sellers who transact business at $200 per contract, as shown in Figure 11.2. If each customer trades one contract, then there are a total of eight transactions (four buys and four sells) and the open interest is four contracts.

FIGURE 11.2

Initial Option Contracts Created

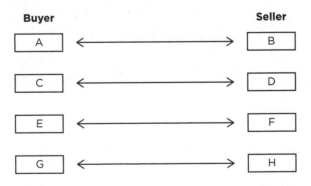

Shortly after initiating the above positions, party E decides to close out the position. Since E initially bought a contract, to close out the position E sells one contract. The difference between the purchase and sale price, if any, is E's profit or loss. If E sells to a buyer without an existing position, then the new buyer (I) just substitutes for E, as shown in Figure 11.3. There are two transactions, one buy and one sell—but the open interest remains the same.

FIGURE 11.3

If Investor I Is Replaced

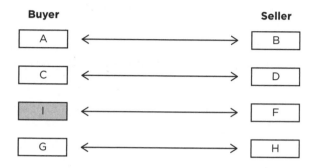

On the other hand, suppose E sells a contract (closing out its long position) and D buys a contract (closing out its short position), as shown in Figure 11.4. Because E sells to a buyer who has an existing short position, the open interest will decline by one. Thus, a rising transaction volume can result in fewer open contracts. Often, as the contract approaches maturity, transactions increase, but the open interest decreases.

FIGURE 11.4

If Investor I and D Close Out with Each Other

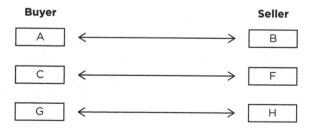

Open interest is the best measure of liquidity—the higher the open interest, the greater the chance that when one investor wants to sell a contract, another investor will want to buy it. The greater the liquidity, the more trades can be done client to client, instead of client to market maker. Client-to-client trades can be done at better prices and result in less price volatility.

MONEYNESS, INTRINSIC VALUE, AND TIME VALUE

Options that would have value if they were exercised immediately are said to have intrinsic value or to be "in the money," as shown in Figure 11.5. Calls with strike prices below the underlying's market value and puts with strike prices above the underlying's market value are "in the money."

FIGURE 11.5

In, at, and out of the Money

	In the Money	At the Money	Out of the Money
Calls	K < M	K ≈ M	K > M
Puts	K > M	K ≈ M	K < M
K = Strike Price		M = Market Value	

For example, suppose a stock is selling for $100.00 and the call prices are as shown in Figure 11.6. The maturity of the options is 1, 4, 7, and 10 months with strike prices from $85 to $115.

FIGURE 11.6

Option Prices

	Calls	Maturity			
		1M	4M	7M	10M
Strike Prices	$85	$15.50	$21.00	$22.00	$24.75
	$90	$11.00	$15.50	$18.00	$20.00
	$95	$6.50	$11.75	$13.75	$15.25
	$100	$4.50	$7.00	$8.50	$9.50
	$105	$1.50	$5.00	$6.50	$7.00
	$110	$0.50	$3.25	$4.00	$5.00
	$115	$0.25	$1.00	$1.25	$1.50

The options with strike prices below $100 are in the money and have intrinsic value. The:

- $85 calls have $15.00 intrinsic value.
- $90 calls have $10.00 intrinsic value.
- $95 calls have $5.00 intrinsic value.
- $100 calls have $0.00 intrinsic value.
- $105 calls have $0.00 intrinsic value.

The option's premium minus the intrinsic value is equal to the option's time value:

The 4M $90 call has a premium of $15.50.
$15.50 minus $10 intrinsic value equals $5.50 time value.

The 7M $110 call has a premium of $4.00.
$4.00 minus $0 intrinsic value equals $4.00 time value.

Exercise Set XXX

Assume XYZ = $100

Calls

	1M	4M	7M	10M
$85	$15.50	$21.00	$22.00	$24.75
$90	$11.00	$15.50	$18.00	$20.00
$95	$6.50	$11.75	$13.75	$15.25
$100	$4.50	$7.00	$8.50	$9.50
$105	$1.50	$5.00	$6.50	$7.00
$110	$0.50	$3.25	$4.00	$5.00
$115	$0.25	$1.00	$1.25	$1.50

Puts

	1M	4M	7M	10M
$85	$0.10	$0.85	$1.00	$1.25
$90	$0.25	$3.00	$3.50	$4.50
$95	$1.00	$4.00	$5.50	$6.00
$100	$4.00	$6.50	$8.00	$8.75
$105	$6.00	$11.25	$13.00	$14.00
$110	$10.00	$15.00	$17.25	$19.00
$115	$14.50	$20.25	$21.00	$23.50

Assuming the following transaction cost schedule (per contract):

Number of Contracts	Transaction Cost
1–4	$20
5–9	$15
10–24	$10
25–49	$7
49–99	$5
100–499	$4
>500[1]	$6

1. Note that over 500 contracts, the transaction cost rises due to a lack of liquidity.

PROBLEM SET 1

- What is the total cost of one 4M IBM ATM call?
- What is the most you can make?
- What is the most you can lose?
- What is the break-even price of the above transaction?
- What is the option's intrinsic value?
- What is the option's time value?

Cost = (# options × price option × $100) + TC =
   (1 × $7 × $100) + $20 = $720

Most you can make = unlimited

Most you can lose = $720

Breakeven = $107.20

Intrinsic value = $0

Time value = $7.00

PROBLEM SET 2

- What is the total cost of 25 7M IBM 90 calls?
- What is the most you can make?
- What is the most you can lose?
- What is the break-even price of the above transaction?
- What is the option's intrinsic value?
- What is the option's time value?

Cost = (# options × price option × $100) + TC =
   (25 × $18 × $100) + (25 × $7) = $45,175

Most you can make = unlimited

Most you can lose = $45,175

Breakeven = $90 + ($45,175 / 2,500) = $108.07

Intrinsic value = $10

Time value = $8.00

PROBLEM SET 3

- What is the total cost of 75 10-month IBM ATM puts?
- What is the most you can make?
- What is the most you can lose?
- What is the break-even price of the above transaction?
- What is the option's intrinsic value?
- What is the option's time value?

Cost = (# options × price option × $100) + TC =
   (75 × $8.75 × $100) + (75 × $5) = $66,000

Most you can make = $750,000 − $66,000 = $684,000

Most you can lose = $66,000

Breakeven = $100 − $8.80 = $91.20

Intrinsic value = $0

Time value = $8.75

PROBLEM SET 4

- What is the total cost if you buy 100 ATM 4M calls and buy 100 ATM 4M puts?
- What is the most you can make?
- What is the most you can lose?
- What is the break-even price of the above transaction?
- What is the option's intrinsic value?
- What is the option's time value?

Cost = (# options × price option × $100) + TC
(100 × $7.00 × $100) + (100 × $4) = $70,400
(100 × $6.50 × $100) + (100 × $4) = $65,400 = $135,800
Most you can make = unlimited
Most you can lose = $135,800
Breakeven = $113.58 and $86.42
Intrinsic value = $0
Time value = $13.50

PROBLEM SET 5

- What is the total cost if you sell 100 ATM 7M calls and sell 100 ATM 4M puts?
- What is the most you can make?
- What is the most you can lose?
- What is the break-even price of the above transaction?
- What is the option's intrinsic value?
- What is the option's time value?

Cost = (# options × price option × $100) + TC
(100 × $8.50 × $100) − (100 × $4) = $84,600
(100 × $6.50 × $100) − (100 × $4) = $64,600 =
    $149,200 (profit)

Most you can make = $149,200

Most you can lose = unlimited

Breakeven = $114.92 and $85.08

Intrinsic value = $0

Time value = $15.00

PROBLEM SET 6

- What is the total cost if you buy 50 ATM 4-month calls and sell 50 ATM 4-month puts?
- What is the most you can make?
- What is the most you can lose?
- What is the break-even price of the above transaction?
- What is the option's intrinsic value?
- What is the option's time value?

Cost = (# options × price option × $100) + TC

(50 × $7.00 × $100) + (50 × $5) = $35,250

(50 × $6.50 × $100) − (50 × $5) = −$32,250 = $3,000

Most you can make = unlimited

Most you can lose = $503,000

Breakeven = $3,000 / $5,000 = $100.60

Intrinsic value = $0

Time value = $13.50

PROBLEM SET 7

- What is the total cost if you buy 100 ATM 4M calls and sell 100 ATM 7M calls?
- What is the most you can make?
- What is the most you can lose?
- What is the break-even price of the above transaction?
- What is the option's intrinsic value?
- What is the option's time value?

Cost = (# options × price option × $100) + TC

(100 × $7.00 × $100) + (100 × $4) = $70,400

− [(100 × $8.50 × $100) − (100 × $4)] = −$84,600 =

   −$14,200 (profit)

Most you can make = 14,200

Most you can lose = unlimited

Breakeven = $101.42

Intrinsic value = $0

Time value = $15.50

PROBLEM SET 8

- What is the total cost if you buy 10,000 shares of stock and sell 100 of the 7M 105 calls?
- What is the most you can make and lose?
- What is the break-even price of the above transaction?
- What is the option's intrinsic value?
- What is the option's time value?

Cost = ($1,000,000 stock − (100 × $6.50 × $100) +

   (100 × $4) = $935,400

Most you can make = $1,050,000 − $935,400 =

   $114,600

Most you can lose = $935,400

Breakeven = $100 − $6.5 + $.04 = $93.54

Intrinsic value = $0

Time value = $6.50

OVER-THE-COUNTER OPTIONS

Unlike listed options, OTC options are private contracts between dealers and customers. They are completely flexible with regard to size of contract, expiration date, strike price, and so forth. One frequent difference between listed and OTC options is dividend protection. Let's look at an example.

It is 2 weeks before a $200 call option on XYZ Inc. expires. The stock is selling at $202 and the option has $2 of intrinsic value. Unfortunately, the stock goes ex-dividend on a $4 dividend payment, and the stock price drops by $4 to $198, where it stays until the option expires. The dividend payment depressed the stock price below the strike price—making the option worthless upon expiration.

If the option was dividend protected, the $4 stock dividend would cause the strike price to drop from $200 to $196. If 2 weeks later the stock was at $198, the option would be worth $2.00 at expiration. Listed options are not dividend protected. OTC options may be dividend protected.

The downside of OTC options is counterparty risk. Both parties can take steps to reduce counterparty risk. For example, if a dealer is worried about a customer's credit quality, the dealer can:

- Adjust the price of the option to incorporate credit risk
- Require the client post collateral
- Mark the client's account to the market so the client has to settle any loses each day
- Include a "cancellation clause" that terminates the contract if the client's credit quality declines

If the customer is worried about the dealer's credit quality, the customer can:

- Diversify counterparties by spreading its business among numerous dealers

- Monitor the credit quality of its dealers
- Have a greater credit exposure *to* the dealer than *from* the dealer

SYNTHETIC POSITIONS AND HEDGING

When a dealer creates an OTC option for a client, the dealer needs to hedge the risk. Unlike listed options and exchanges, the dealers probably won't have an identical option on which it takes the other side of the trade. The dealer will have to create a synthetic offsetting position in order to hedge the exposures it creates when it creates OTC options. Figure 11.7 describes these offsetting positions.

FIGURE 11.7
Synthetic Positions

Position	Synthetic Position
Long call	Long put and long underlying
Long put	Long call and short underlying
Short call	Short underlying and short put
Short put	Long underlying and short call
Long stock	Long call and short put
Short stock	Long put and short call

Often, the prices the dealers charge for options depend upon what it costs them to hedge the risk.

EUROPEAN OPTION PUT-CALL PARITY

The value of a call (the premium) is equal to its intrinsic value plus its time value. The intrinsic value is the greater of "MV − K" and "0":

The time value is equal to "leverage" and "choice."

The "leverage" is a positive because owning a call option allows an investor to delay the expenditure of cash to buy the underlying until expiration date. A 3-month call on IBM common allows the long to benefit from rises in the price of IBM common, and yet delays the outlay of cash to acquire the stock by 3 months. Thus, the benefit of leverage is K − PV(k).

The "choice" is also a positive because the long can choose to enforce the contract or ignore it when that is to the long's advantage. The long will use the option if it is in the money on expiration date—and cancel the option if it is out of the money. If a call option had a strike of $200 and the market value at expiration was $190, the ability to cancel the contract is worth $10. This is also the price of a put. Thus, the value of "choice" is equal to the value of a put.

Putting it all together:

Call value = intrinsic value + time value

Call value = Max(MV-k, 0) + leverage + choice

Call value = Max(MV-k, 0) + K-PV(k) + put

Call value = MV − PV(k) + put

EXAMPLE 1

Given the below data, calculate the value of a put.

Call price = $15

Strike price = $100

Interest rate = 8% cc 30/360

Expiration = 1 year

Market value = $105

Call value = MV − PV(k) + put

$15 = $105.00 − $100e$^{(-.08 \times 1)}$ + put

$15 = $105.00 − $92.31 + put

−$90 = −$92.31 + put

Put = $2.31

Dividends reduce the market value, so the formula for stocks that pay a dividend is:

Call value = MV − PV(div) − PV(k) + put

Dividends can be continuous (index) or discrete individual stock. Continuous dividends should be present valued from the midpoint of the option's life. Discrete dividends should be discounted from the actual ex-dividend dates since those are the days when the party receiving the dividend is determined.

EXAMPLE 2

Given the above data, recalculate the value of a put assuming the index pays a 5% continuous dividend.

Call value = MV − PV(div) − PV(k) + put

$15 = $105.00 − $5e$^{(-.08 \times .5)}$ − $100e$^{(-.08 \times 1)}$ + put

$15 = $105.00 − $4.80 − $92.31 + put

−$90 = −$97.11 + put

Put = $7.11

Q: Suppose the put was selling for $8.00, what is the market saying about the future dividend rate?

A: If the put was selling for $8.00, it means investors expect the dividend to be raised. If they are raised, the stocks will decline further on the X-dividend days and the put will be more valuable.

EXAMPLE 3

Given the above data, recalculate the value of a put assuming a $2.00 dividend in 2, 5, 8, and 11 months 30/360. Interest rates are 4%, 6%, 8%, and 8%, respectively.

Step 1 PV the dividends = $7.70

$2.00 / (1 + (.04 × 60 / 360)) = $1.99

$2.00 / (1 + (.06 × 150 / 360)) = $1.95

$2.00 / (1 + (.08 × 240 / 360)) = $1.90

$2.00 / (1 + (.08 × 330 / 360)) = $1.86

Call value = MV − PV(div) − PV(k) + put

$15 = $105.00 − $7.70 − $100e^{(-.08 \times 1)} + put

$15 = $105.00 − $7.70 − $92.31 + put

−$90 = −$7.70 − $92.31 + put

−90 = −100.01 + put

Put = $10.01

CHAPTER TWELVE

Option Pricing

Understanding how options are priced is essential for serious investors—even if they are going to rely on computer models to do the actual pricing. The reason investors need to understand option pricing is that it is the key to:

- Establishing and maintaining valid hedges that use options
- Doing relative value analysis between different options, and options vs. the underlying
- Understanding the option sensitivities
- Understanding the various option strategies
- Understanding long-dated options like LEAPS (Long-term Equity Appreciation Securities) and warrants
- Understanding convertible bonds/reverse converts and other debt equity hybrids

For the purposes of pricing, options are raffle tickets. Like all raffle tickets, their value is:

Value of a raffle ticket = PV (potential prize × probability
of winning)

EXAMPLE ONE
*Prize $100,000, 10 tickets sold, winner announced in a year,
interest rate 10%*
Value of a raffle ticket = ($100,000 × 10%) / (1 + .1) =
$9,090.91 today and $10,000 in a year

When this model is translated to options, you find that:

- The potential prize equates to the intrinsic value at expiration.
- The probability of winning equates to the probability that the
  option will be in the money at expiration.

LOGNORMAL DISTRIBUTION PRICING MODEL

To estimate whether there will be any intrinsic value at expiration
(and if so, how much) requires building a model. As with all pricing models, the more assumptions its designers make, the simpler
the model is to build. The lognormal distribution pricing model
includes a number of assumptions:

Continuous trading—The assumption that the underlying
instrument trades continuously (24 hours a day, 365 days
a year) is reasonable for some underlying instruments, like
the major currency pairs (EUR/USD, JPY/USD, GBP/
USD), major commodities (oil, gold), and major stock indices (S&P 500, FTSE 100). The assumption is not reason-

able for a thinly traded OTC stock—and so neither is the lognormal distribution pricing model.

Infinite infinitely small price moves—The assumption that the price of the underlying changes in an infinite number of infinitely small price moves is not strictly true for any underlying. It is reasonably true for very liquid underlying instruments where the bid-ask spread is tiny relative to the price of the underlying and large trades do not cause price jumps.

Underlying price reflects all known information—The model assumes that the price of the underlying accurately reflects all known information. Since the current price reflects all known information, the only thing that causes the price to change is new information—which is, by definition, unknown. Since this new information is random, the underlying's price movements in the future will be random.

Past prices do not impact future prices—If this assumption is true, then the entire field of technical analysis is worthless. It has been demonstrated that technical analysis adds value at least over the short term, so the lognormal pricing distribution model is only good for options that have more than a month left until expiration.

Past volatility indicates future volatility—The lognormal pricing distribution model assumes that past volatility of a stock is indicative of future volatility. If the market has trouble reaching a consensus on what the future earnings of a company will be or how available a commodity will be, the price of the stock or commodity will be volatile as the market reacts and overreacts to each new piece of information. Also, a lack of consensus often results in the stock or commodity being held in "weak hands" that will reverse their position with each news announcement.

Future returns are normally distributed—Here the assumption is that the distribution of future returns, not future prices, is normally distributed. If the future prices were normally distributed, that would create two problems:

- First, if the stock was currently selling for $100 and the distribution 1 year from now was normally distributed around $100, there would be an equal probability of a gain and a loss. Also, the magnitude of the potential gains would equal the magnitude of the potential losses. If the size of the gains and losses is the same, and the probability of gain and loss is the same, the potential gains and losses in a year are equal. However, when you factor in transaction charges, both longs and shorts must lose over the long term. This is not a model for investing; it is the model that built Las Vegas.

- Second, suppose that the mean was $100 and the standard deviation was $40. In this case the distribution of future prices would look like the one depicted in Figure 12.1. The problem is that this distribution includes negative values, which are impossible for stocks, bonds, and commodities.

FIGURE 12.1

Normal Distribution

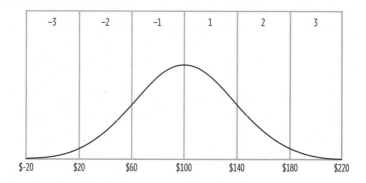

If, however, we assume that the returns (instead of the prices) are normally distributed, then 10% gains and 10% losses are equally likely—as are two successive 10% gains and two successive 10% losses. In this event, a $21 gain has the same probability of occurring as a $19 loss. Ten percent gains, ad infinitum, cause the price to approach infinity, while 10% losses, ad infinitum, cause the price to approach $0. Both are consistent with what we know about the possible price range of stocks and commodities, as you can see in Figure 12.2.

FIGURE 12.2

Impact of Successive Fixed Percent Gains and Losses

						$100								
					-10%		+10%							
				$90				$110						
			-10%						+10%					
		$89								$121				
	. . .										. . .			
	-10%											+10%		
. . .													. . .	
$0														∞

Risk-free rate is both known and fixed—The risk-free rate is a concept. In the US, the Treasury spot rate serves as a reasonable surrogate. Even though Treasuries have some credit risk, it is minimal so that the error introduced is negligible. However, the Treasury spot rates are not fixed, but as they change so will the value of the option.

Everyone can borrow and invest at the risk-free rate—While everyone can invest at the Treasury rate, not everyone can borrow at the risk-free.

Finally, the lognormal pricing distribution model assumes that:

- There are no transaction costs.
- There are no dividends.
- Option has European expiration.
- Life of the underlying cannot be changed due to call, put, merger, etc.
- Delivery process is fair and unbiased.

Given these assumptions, the formula that explains the behavior of the underlying is:

$$\Delta S = \mu \Delta t + \sigma \varepsilon \sqrt{\Delta t}$$

S = the stock's price

μ = the risk-free rate

σ = the stock's volatility

ε = normal curve with a mean of 0 and standard deviation of 1

t = time until expiration

EXAMPLE 1

Market value = $100

Strike price = $100

Volatility = 20%

Expiration = 1 year

Risk-free rate = 5%

$$\Delta S = .05(1) + .2\varepsilon(1)$$
$$\Delta S = .05 + .2\varepsilon$$

This equation is then solved a "statically infinite" number of times. To solve the equation a value is selected at random from a standardized normal curve (mean = 0, standard deviation = 1). Naturally, the value "0" and values close to it will be selected most often. As with any normal curve, the probability of randomly selecting a result between:

- 1 and −1 standard deviations is approximately 67%
- 2 and −2 standard deviations is approximately 96%
- 3 and −3 standard deviations is approximately 99+%

Also, the probability of randomly selecting a value of +1 standard deviations from the mean is equal to the probability of randomly selecting a value of −1 standard deviations from the mean. The information presented in Figure 12.3 depicts the results of selecting random values and plugging them into the equation in order to estimate the future price. (Note that only whole numbers were used; in practice, numbers would be selected out to 4 to 6 decimal places.)

FIGURE 12.3

Price of Underlying

Value Selected from Curve	Resulting Equation	Equation Result	Price of Underlying
0	$\Delta S = .05 + .2(0)$	+05%	$105
+1	$\Delta S = .05 + .2(+1)$	+25%	$125
−1	$\Delta S = .05 + .2(−1)$	−15%	$85
+2	$\Delta S = .05 + .2(+2)$	+45%	$145
−2	$\Delta S = .05 + .2(−2)$	−35%	$65
+3	$\Delta S = .05 + .2(+3)$	+65%	$165
−3	$\Delta S = .05 + .2(−3)$	−55%	$45

The results (the possible future prices) are then plotted. As more and more results are added, the stacks start to grow; the dots become smaller and then coalesce, as shown in Figure 12.4.

FIGURE 12.4

Start Plotting the Results

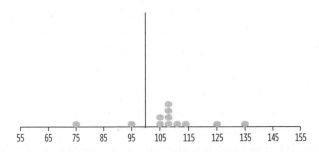

As the number of results added to the graph is increased, the shape of the distribution of future prices becomes clearer and clearer (see Figure 12.5 and Figure 12.6).

FIGURE 12.5

Continue Plotting the Results

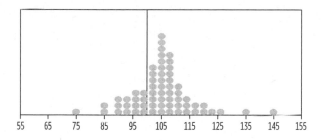

FIGURE 12.6

Continue Plotting the Results

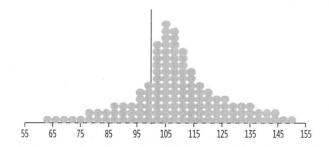

As the number of results increases, the shape becomes smoother and eventually you end up with a lognormal distribution of possible prices in a year, as shown in Figure 12.7. Because the assumption that the price changes in an infinite number of small price changes was made up front, the resulting curve is continuous. Note that because the curve is lognormal, there is a bias toward the upside. The average move up exceeds the average more down. The probability of an up move also exceeds the probability of a down move.

FIGURE 12.7

Resulting Lognormal Curve

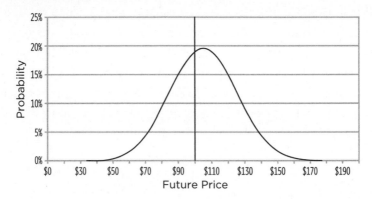

The advantage of having a continuous curve is that it makes it simple to answer the questions that need to be answered to value the options; namely:

- What will the option's intrinsic value be at expiration?
- What is the probability that the option will have any intrinsic value at expiration?

The intrinsic value at expiration for an at-the-money $100 call would be MV – $100. Thus, in a year, if the stock is selling for:

- $101, the intrinsic value would be $1
- $102, the intrinsic value would be $2
- $105, the intrinsic value would be $5
- $110, the intrinsic value would be $10
- $150, the intrinsic value would be $50

It is impossible to know, in advance, what the intrinsic value will be. However, we do know what the probability is that the intrinsic value will be $1, $2, $3, . . . $50, . . . $70, . . . etc.

Since the probability of each intrinsic value is known, we can calculate a weighted average of the various possible intrinsic values. This weighted average can be expressed as a multiple of the spot price. This multiple, is called the "up factor" (U). This is the "average" amount by which the S price will rise over a time frame given its volatility. Of course, the price could rise by more, rise by less, or not rise at all. Multiplying S and U together produces the weighted average (weighted by probability) of all the prices higher than the spot price.

$$SU = Se^{\sigma\sqrt{\Delta t}} = \$100 \times e^{2\sqrt{1}} = \$100 \times 1.2214 = \$122.14$$

$$SU = Se^{\sigma\sqrt{t}} = Se^{.2\sqrt{1}}$$

$$\$100 \times (1.2214) = \$122.14$$

In Figure 12.8, $122.14 is the weighted average of the shaded region.

FIGURE 12.8

Weighted Average of Higher Prices

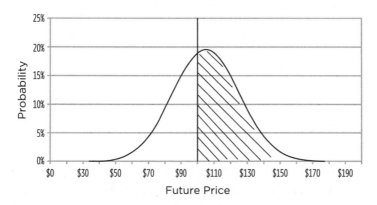

The weighted average of the prices that are lower than spot can be found by calculating the "D" factor and multiplying it by spot.

$$SD = Se^{-\sigma\sqrt{t}} = \$100 \times e^{-.2\sqrt{t}} = \$100 \times 81.87 = \$81.87$$

or

$$\frac{1}{1.2214} = .8187$$

$$SU = Se^{-\sigma\sqrt{\Delta t}} = Se^{-.2\sqrt{t}}$$

$$\$100 \times (.8187) = \$81.87$$

$$\frac{1}{1.2214} = \$81.87$$

Note that while the average up move is $22.14, the average down move is $18.13. This is because of the upward bias inherent in a lognormal distribution. It is also one of the reasons why an ATM call has a greater value than an ATM put.

FIGURE 12.9

Weighted Average of Lower Prices

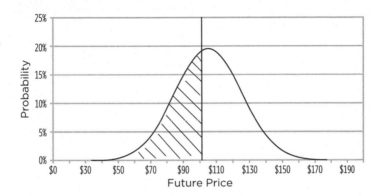

The second question, what is the probability that the call or put option will be in the money can be answered by solving for the probability up (P_u). The U and D are the same as we discussed earlier. Once the probability of an up move is calculated, the probability of a down move (P_d) is simply: $1 - P_u$.

$$P_u = 57.75\% \text{ so } P_d = 1 - 57.75\% = 42.25\%$$

$$P_u = \frac{e^{rt} - D}{U - D}$$

$$P_u = \frac{1.0517 - .8187}{1.2214 - .8187}$$

$$P_u = 57.75\%$$

These four numbers (U, D, P_u, and P_d) are a shorthand way of describing the entire lognormal curve and are all that is necessary to value ATM options. (See Figure 12.10 and Figure 12.11.) Consider the following:

Value of a raffle ticket = PV (potential prize × probability of winning)

Value of an ATM call = PV (average intrinsic value above spot × probability of up move)

Value of an ATM put = PV (average intrinsic value below spot × probability of down move)

FIGURE 12.10

Probability of Price Going Up

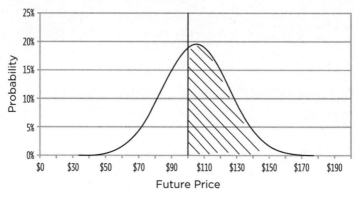

FIGURE 12.11

Calculation of ATM Call and Put

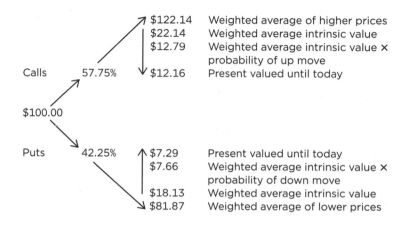

	$122.14	Weighted average of higher prices
	$22.14	Weighted average intrinsic value
	$12.79	Weighted average intrinsic value × probability of up move
Calls 57.75%	$12.16	Present valued until today
$100.00		
Puts 42.25%	$7.29	Present valued until today
	$7.66	Weighted average intrinsic value × probability of down move
	$18.13	Weighted average intrinsic value
	$81.87	Weighted average of lower prices

Starting at $100, if the stock goes up, it will go up (on average) to $122.14. That means the average intrinsic value at expiration (the average "win") is $22.14. Of course, there is only a 57.75% chance of having a winning ticket, thus the option is only worth $12.79 (weighted average intrinsic value × probability of up move) in a year. It is worth the present value of $12.29 today – ($12.79^{e -.05}$) = $12.16.

As another example, suppose Palladium is selling for $500, its historic volatility is 25%, and the risk-free rate is 8.00% cc 30/360. Let's price the 6-month ATM call and put, as shown in Figure 12.12. Going right to the calculation of the four values that abbreviate the entire lognormal curve:

$$U = e^{.25\sqrt{.5}} = 1.1934 \times \$500 = \$596.68$$
$$D = e^{-.25\sqrt{.5}} = .8380 \times \$500 = \$418.98$$
$$P_u = \frac{e^{(08).5} - D}{U - D} = 57.075\%$$
$$P_d = 42.925\%$$

FIGURE 12.12

Calculation of ATM Call and Put

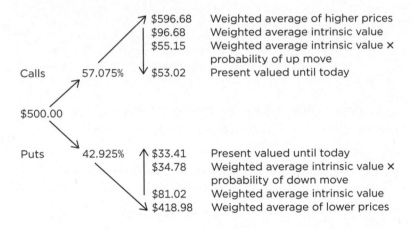

As a final example, suppose the current risk-free rate is 5.00% cc 30/360 and its annual volatility is 15%. Use this information and the equations that follow to determine the price of an ATM 6-month call and put. (See Figure 12.13.)

$$U = e^{.15\sqrt{.5}} = 1.11189528$$
$$D = e^{-.15\sqrt{.5}} = .89936527$$
$$P_u = \frac{e^{(.05).5} - D}{U - D} = 59.26\%$$
$$P_d = 40.74\%$$

FIGURE 12.13

Calculation of ATM Call and Put on Rates

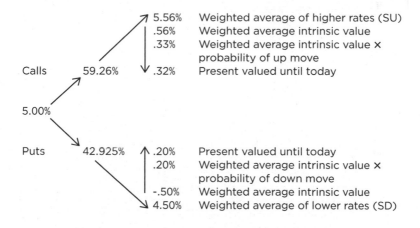

		5.56%	Weighted average of higher rates (SU)
		.56%	Weighted average intrinsic value
		.33%	Weighted average intrinsic value × probability of up move
Calls	59.26%	.32%	Present valued until today
5.00%			
Puts	42.925%	.20%	Present valued until today
		.20%	Weighted average intrinsic value × probability of down move
		-.50%	Weighted average intrinsic value
		4.50%	Weighted average of lower rates (SD)

BINOMIAL MODELS

The problem with the lognormal distribution model is that, while it can be used to value options on stocks, commodities, or interest rates, it can only value ATM options. The only data the model generates is the probability of up moves and down moves from spot. The only intrinsic values are measured from spot.

Investors want to value options across a broad range of strike prices—not just ATM options. To do this, they need to break time down into smaller intervals. By doing so, the binomial model generates more data that can then be used to value any option.

With time broken into smaller intervals, a price tree can be built, as shown in Figure 12.14. U and D are calculated as before—but just with a shorter time frame. The price at each node in the tree is simple: the spot price times the number of U factors and D factors to reach the node.

FIGURE 12.14

The Price Tree

					SU^5
				SU^4	
			SU^3		SU^4D^1
		SU^2		SU^3D^1	
	SU^1		SU^2D^1		SU^3D^2
S		SU^1D^1		SU^2D^2	
	SD^1		SU^1D^2		SU^2D^3
		SD^2		SU^1D^3	
			SD^3		SU^1D^4
				SD^4	
					SD^5

However, since U times D = 1, the tree simplifies to the one shown in Figure 12.15, where the values along the edge are replicated in the interior.

FIGURE 12.15

The Simplified Price Tree

					SU^5
				SU^4	
			SU^3		SU^3
		SU^2		SU^2	
	SU^1		SU^1		SU^1
S		S		S	
	SD^1		SD^1		SD^1
		SD^2		SD^2	
			SD^3		SD^3
				SD^4	
					SD^5

The probability of reaching a node in the tree is equal to the probability of each path that leads to that node times the number of paths that lead to that node.

- The probability of *each* path that leads to the node is determined using $P_u X P_d Y$, where:
  - P_u equals the probability of an up move
  - P_d equals the probability of a down move
  - X equals the number of up moves to reach the node
  - Y equals the number of down moves to reach the node
- The number of paths that lead to a node is equal to:

$$\text{\# of paths} = \frac{\text{\# of steps to reach node factorial}}{(\text{\# of up moves factorial}) \times (\text{\# of down moves factorial})}$$

Total probability = number of paths × probability of each path

$$\text{Total probability} = \frac{5!}{3! \times 2!} \times P_u^3 P_d^2$$

Thus, the probability of reaching the 2 node down on the fifth step (see Figure 12.16) would be calculated:

Total probability = number of paths × probability of each
      path

The total probability of reaching each node is:

$$\text{Total probability} = \frac{5!}{3! \times 2!} \; P_u{}^3 P_d{}^2$$

FIGURE 12.16

The Probability Tree

					$P_u{}^5$
				$P_u{}^4$	
			$P_u{}^3$		$5P_u{}^4 P_d{}^1$
		$P_u{}^2$		$4P_u{}^3 P_d{}^1$	
	$P_u{}^1$		$3P_u{}^2 P_d$		$10P_u{}^3 P_d{}^2$
100%		$2P_u{}^1 P_d{}^1$		$6P_u{}^2 P_d{}^2$	
	$P_d{}^1$		$3P_u P_d{}^2$		$10P_u{}^2 P_d{}^3$
		$P_d{}^2$		$4P_u{}^1 P_d{}^3$	
			$P_d{}^3$		$5P_u{}^1 P_d{}^4$
				$P_d{}^4$	
					$P_d{}^5$

If the option has a European expiration, the only values needed to value the option are the last values in the tree. These are the ones to the far right and are referred to as the terminal values.

EXAMPLE PRICING EUROPEAN OPTION USING THE TERMINAL VALUES OF A BINOMIAL MODEL:

Spot = $100

Strike price = $130

Expiration = 1 year
Steps = 12
Annual volatility = 18%
Risk-free rate = 6.00%

Calculate the four lognormal curve surrogates:

$$U = e^{.18\sqrt{\frac{1}{12}}} = 1.05334$$

$$D = e^{-.18\sqrt{\frac{1}{12}}} = .94937$$

$$P_U = e\,\frac{e^{(06)(1/12)} - D}{U - D} = .535224\%$$

$$P_d = .464776$$

In the case in Figure 12.17, the top four values are in the money for a 130 call. Multiplying the total probability of reaching these nodes by the intrinsic value at these nodes gives the value of all four options. Summing them and calculating the PV of the result gives us the value of the call option.

In the case in Figure 12.18, the bottom nine values are in the money for a 130 put. Multiplying the total probability of reaching these nodes by the intrinsic value at these nodes gives the value of all nine options. Summing them and calculating the PV of the result gives us the value of the put option, as shown in Figure 12.18.

FIGURE 12.17

Using Terminal Values to Value Options

# of Up Moves	# of Down Moves	Probability of Each Path	# of Paths	Total Probability	Terminal Value	Intrinsic Value	Option Value
12	0	$P_u^{12}P_d^{0}$ = .05526186%	1	0.06%	$186.55	$56.55	$0.03
11	1	$P_u^{11}P_d^{1}$ = .04798813%	12	0.58%	$168.14	$38.14	$0.22
10	2	$P_u^{10}P_d^{2}$ = .04167180%	66	2.75%	$151.54	$21.54	$0.59
9	3	$P_u^{9}P_d^{3}$ = .03618684%	220	7.96%	$136.58	$6.58	$0.52
8	4	$P_u^{8}P_d^{4}$ = .03142382%	495	15.55%	$123.10	$0.00	TOTAL
7	5	$P_u^{7}P_d^{5}$ = .02728773%	792	21.61%	$110.95	$0.00	$1.37
6	6	$P_u6P_d^{6}$ = .02369604%	924	21.90%	$100.00	$0.00	PV
5	7	$P_u^{5}P_d^{7}$ = .02057710%	796	16.30%	$90.13	$0.00	$1.29
4	8	$P_u^{4}P_d^{8}$ = .01786868%	495	8.84%	$81.23	$0.00	
3	9	$P_u^{3}P_d^{9}$ = .01551675%	220	3.41%	$73.22	$0.00	
2	10	$P_u^{2}P_d^{10}$ = .01347440%	66	0.89%	$65.99	$0.00	
1	11	$P_u^{1}P_d^{11}$ = .01170086%	12	0.14%	$59.48	$0.00	
0	12	$P_u^{0}P_d^{12}$ = .01016076%	1	0.01%	$53.61	$0.00	

FIGURE 12.18

Terminal Values Used to Value Put

# of Up Moves	# of Down Moves	Probability of Each Path	# of Paths	Total Probability	Terminal Value	Intrinsic Value	Option Value
12	0	$P_u^{12}P_d^0 = .05526186\%$	1	.06%	$186.55	$ 0.00	$23.72
11	1	$P_u^{11}P_d^1 = .04798813\%$	12	.58%	$168.14	$ 0.00	PV
10	2	$P_u^{10}P_d^2 = .04167180\%$	66	2.75%	$151.54	$ 0.00	$25.18
9	3	$P_u^9P_d^3 = .03618684\%$	220	7.96%	$136.58	$0.00	Total
8	4	$P_u^8P_d^4 = .03142382\%$	495	15.55%	$123.10	$6.90	$1.07
7	5	$P_u^7P_d^5 = .02728773\%$	792	21.61%	$110.95	$19.05	$4.12
6	6	$P_u^6P_d^6 = .02369604\%$	924	21.90%	$100.00	$30.00	$6.57
5	7	$P_u^5P_d^7 = .02057710\%$	796	16.30%	$90.13	$39.87	$6.50
4	8	$P_u^4P_d^8 = .01786868\%$	495	8.84%	$81.23	$48.77	$4.31
3	9	$P_u^3P_d^9 = .01551675\%$	220	3.41%	$73.22	$56.78	$1.94
2	10	$P_u^2P_d^{10} = .01347440\%$	66	.89%	$65.99	$64.01	$0.57
1	11	$P_u^1P_d^{11} = .01170086\%$	12	.14%	$59.48	$70.52	$0.10
0	12	$P_u^0P_d^{12} = .01016076\%$	1	.01%	$53.61	$76.39	$0.01

Relative Value of American vs. European Options

American and European options can either have the same value—or different values—depending on the type of option and whether or not the underlying generates cash flows. Consider the below categories:

- Underlyings that don't pay dividends:
  - *Calls*—For non-dividend-paying stocks, it never makes sense to exercise a fairly valued option early. Exercising the option gives the "long" the intrinsic value—but any time value is lost. Thus, if the long wants to get out of the position, the long should sell—not exercise. Since exercising early offers no value, American and European calls on non-dividend-paying stocks should be equally priced.
  - *Puts*—For non-dividend-paying stocks, it often makes sense to exercise a fairly valued option early. Exercising the option gives the "short" the time value of money—but choice is lost. If the time value of money is greater than the value of choice, it makes sense to exercise early. Since exercising early can offer value, American puts should be worth more than comparable European puts.
- Underlyings that pay dividends:
  - *Calls*—If the present value of the dividends exceeds the option's time value, it can make sense to exercise early. Therefore, American calls can be more valuable than European calls.
  - *Puts*—If the gain from the time value of money exceeds "time value + PV dividends," exercising early can be valu-

able, so American puts can be worth more than comparable European puts.

To quantify the value of being able to exercise early, it is necessary to price the option by stepping back through the tree. Start with the terminal values and then work back to the previous nodes. At each node:

- Calculate the value of the option assuming it will be held for another step. The formula will be:

$$\text{Option Value} = \frac{[\text{Higher Value} \times P_u] + [\text{Lower Value} \times P_d]}{e^{rt}}$$

- Calculate the value of the option if it is exercised:

Max[MV-S,0] for a call
Max[S-MV,0] for a put

Enter whichever value is greater for the node. Repeat for the next node, and continue stepping back until the tree reaches its start.

EXAMPLE
Market value = $100
Strike = $100
Volatility = 20%
Expiration = 1 year
Rate = 5%
Steps = 6

Start by calculating the four values that serve as surrogates for the curve:

U = 1.085075596
D = .921594775
P_u = .530786282
P_d = .469213718

Figure 12.19 shows the use of terminal values to calculate the value of a European put. Figure 12.20 depicts the tree used to value the European put, and Figure 12.21 shows working through a tree European put. By comparison, Figure 12.22 depicts an American put valuation.

FIGURE 12.19

Using Terminal Values to Value European Put

Up Moves	Down Moves	Tree Price	Intrinsic Value	Total Probability	Put Value
6	0	$163.21	$0	2.2362%	$0
5	1	$138.62	$0	11.8619%	$0
4	2	$117.74	$0	26.2127%	$0
3	3	$100.00	$0	30.8959%	$0
2	4	$84.93	$15.07	20.4839%	$3.09
1	5	$74.14	$25.86	7.2431%	$2.02
0	6	$61.27	$38.73	1.0671%	$0.41
				Sum	$5.52
				PV	$5.25

FIGURE 12.20

Tree to Value European Put

						$163.21
					$150.42	
				$138.62		$138.62
			$127.76		$127.76	
		$117.74		$117.74		$117.74
	$108.51		$108.51		$108.51	
$100.00		$100.00		$100.00		$100.00
	$92.16		$92.16		$92.16	
		$84.93		$84.93		$84.93
			$78.27		$78.27	
				$72.14		$72.14
					$66.48	
						$61.27

FIGURE 12.21

Working Through Tree European Put

						$0.00
					$0.00	
				$0.00		$0.00
			$0.00		$0.00	
		$0.71		$0.00		$0.00
	$2.47		$1.52		$0.00	
$5.25		$4.50		$3.26		$0.00
	$8.49		$7.96		$7.01	
		$13.15		$13.41		$15.07
			$19.26		$20.90	
				$26.21		$27.86
					$32.69	
						$38.73

FIGURE 12.22

American Put Valuation

						$0.00
					$0.00	
				$0.00		$0.00
			$0.00		$0.00	
		$0.79		$0.00		$0.00
	$2.77		$1.70		$0.00	
$5.95		$5.05		$3.65		$0.00
	$9.67		$8.93		$7.84	
		$15.07		$15.07		$15.07
			$21.73		$21.73	
				$27.86		$27.86
					$33.52	
						$38.73

For the European put, the value is the same regardless of whether the terminal values are used or the values are walked back through the tree. Since the European option can't be exercised early, the value at each node is the discounted weighted average of the next two possible values in the tree. For the American put, the value is the greater of intrinsic value or the discounted weighted average of the next two possible values in the tree. The value of being able to exercise early is equal to the difference in value between the options: ($5.95 − $5.25) = $0.70.

To summarize this model, known as the Cox Ross Rubinstein model:

$$U = e^{\sigma\sqrt{t}}$$

$$D = e^{-\sigma\sqrt{t}} = 1/U$$

$$P_u = e\ \frac{e^{rt} - D}{U - D}$$

$$P_d = e\ (1 - P_u)$$

$$SUD = S$$

Price at any node $= SU^xD^y$

Probability $=$ [number of paths] $\times$ [probability of each path]

$$\text{Probability} = \left[\frac{\#\text{ of steps!}}{(X!)(Y!)}\right] \times \left[(P_u)^x\ (1 - P_u)^y\right]$$

Forward Price Pricing Model

The forward price pricing model is an alternative model for pricing options that doesn't rely on the assumption of a lognormal curve distributed around the current price. Instead, it assumes:

- A normal distribution of future prices around the forward price.
- The prices recombine at the forward price at each step.
- The time period and volatility are constants.
- Each step has a 50% up probability and a 50% down probability.

To summarize this model:

$$U = \frac{2e^{\mu\Delta t 2\sigma\sqrt{\Delta t}}}{e^{2\sigma\sqrt{t}} + 1}$$

$$D = \frac{2e^{\mu\Delta t}}{e^{2\sigma\sqrt{t}} + 1}$$

$$pSu + (1 - p)Sd = S_0 e^{rt}$$

thus:

$$P_u = e\,\frac{e^{rt} - D}{U - D}$$

$$U/D = e^{2\sigma\sqrt{\Delta t}}$$

$$U/D = Se^{2\mu\Delta t}$$

Price at any node = SU^xD^y

Probability = [number of paths] × [probability of each path]

$$\text{Probability} = \left[\frac{\# \text{ of steps!}}{(X!)(Y!)}\right] \times \left[(P_u)^x\,(1 - P_u)^y\right]$$

FIGURE 12.23

Forward-Centering Binomial Model

Spot = $100
Strike price for call and put = $130
Expiration = 1 year
Steps = 12
Annual volatility = 18%
Risk-free rate = 6%

U = 1.059434237
D = .943900022
P_u = .521709843
P_d = .478290157

# of Up Moves	# of Down Moves	# of Paths	Probability of Each Path	Total Probability	Price	Call Value	Put Value
12	0	1	.04065822%	.0407%	$199.93	$69.93	$0.00
11	1	12	.03727441%	.4473%	$178.13	$48.13	$0.00
10	2	66	.03417222%	2.2554%	$158.71	$28.71	$0.00
9	3	220	.03132821%	6.8922%	$141.40	$11.40	$0.00
8	4	495	.02872090%	14.2168%	$125.98	$0.00	$4.02
7	5	792	.02633058%	20.8538%	$112.24	$0.00	$17.76
6	6	924	.02413920%	22.3046%	$100.00	$0.00	$30.00
5	7	792	.02213020%	17.5271%	$89.09	$0.00	$40.91
4	8	495	.02028839%	10.0428%	$79.38	$0.00	$50.62
3	9	220	.01859988%	4.0920%	$70.72	$0.00	$59.28
2	10	66	.01705189%	1.1254%	$63.01	$0.00	$66.99
1	11	12	.01563273%	.1876%	$56.14	$0.00	$73.86
0	12	1	.01433169%	.0143%	$50.02	$0.00	$79.98
					TOTAL	$1.68	$26.55
					PV	$1.59	$25.25

Trinomial Models

In a trinomial model, it is assumed that the price of the underlying instrument can either go up, go down, or stay flat. In effect, it's a binomial model that skips every other step. By having this model, you get more nodes and data points at each step along the tree. For example, at the sixth step a binomial model has seven data points whereas a trinomial model has 13 data points.

The other advantage of trinomial models is that by adjusting the time between steps it is possible to set the tree recombination level at a "barrier" level—making it easier to value a barrier option.

Figure 12.24 introduces the Boyle Trinomial Model, and Figure 12.25 shows the Hull White Model.

FIGURE 12.24

Boyle Trinomial Model

$$U = e^{\sigma\sqrt{2\Delta t}}$$

$$D = e^{-\sigma\sqrt{2\Delta t}}$$

$$P_U = \left[\frac{e^{r\Delta t/2} - e^{-\sigma\sqrt{\Delta t/2}}}{e^{\sigma\sqrt{\Delta t/2}} - e^{-\sigma\sqrt{\Delta t/2}}} \right]^2$$

$$P_d = \left[\frac{e^{\sigma\sqrt{\Delta t/2}} - e^{r\Delta t/2}}{e^{\sigma\sqrt{\Delta t/2}} - e^{-\sigma\sqrt{\Delta t/2}}} \right]^2$$

$$P_m = 1 - (P_U + P_d)$$
$$P^f = ?$$

Spot	$100.00												
Strike	$100.00												
Periods	12												$241.53
Volatility	18%											$224.42	$224.42
Rate	6%										$208.52	$208.52	$208.52
Time	0.083333									$193.74	$193.74	$193.74	$193.74
U	1.076252062								$180.02	$180.02	$180.02	$180.02	$180.02
D	0.929150369							$167.26	$167.26	$167.26	$167.26	$167.26	$167.26
P_u	0.27548960						$155.41	$155.41	$155.41	$155.41	$155.41	$155.41	$155.41
P_f	0.49876286					$144.40	$144.40	$144.40	$144.40	$144.40	$144.40	$144.40	$144.40
P_d	0.225747533				$134.17	$134.17	$134.17	$134.17	$134.17	$134.17	$134.17	$134.17	$134.17
				$124.66	$124.66	$124.66	$124.66	$124.66	$124.66	$124.66	$124.66	$124.66	$124.66
			$115.83	$115.83	$115.83	$115.83	$115.83	$115.83	$115.83	$115.83	$115.83	$115.83	$115.83
		$107.63	$107.63	$107.63	$107.63	$107.63	$107.63	$107.63	$107.63	$107.63	$107.63	$107.63	$107.63
	$100.00	$100.00	$100.00	$100.00	$100.00	$100.00	$100.00	$100.00	$100.00	$100.00	$100.00	$100.00	$100.00
		$92.92	$92.92	$92.92	$92.92	$92.92	$92.92	$92.92	$92.92	$92.92	$92.92	$92.92	$92.92
			$86.33	$86.33	$86.33	$86.33	$86.33	$86.33	$86.33	$86.33	$86.33	$86.33	$86.33
				$80.22	$80.22	$80.22	$80.22	$80.22	$80.22	$80.22	$80.22	$80.22	$80.22
					$74.53	$74.53	$74.53	$74.53	$74.53	$74.53	$74.53	$74.53	$74.53
						$69.25	$69.25	$69.25	$69.25	$69.25	$69.25	$69.25	$69.25
							$64.35	$64.35	$64.35	$64.35	$64.35	$64.35	$64.35
								$59.79	$59.79	$59.79	$59.79	$59.79	$59.79
									$55.55	$55.55	$55.55	$55.55	$55.55
										$51.61	$51.61	$51.61	$51.61
											$47.96	$47.96	$47.96
												$44.56	$44.56
													$41.40
													$141.53
												$124.91	$124.42
											$109.51	$109.02	$108.52
										$95.23	$94.74	$94.24	$93.74
									$82.00	$81.51	$81.01	$80.52	$80.02
								$69.73	$69.24	$68.75	$68.26	$67.76	$67.26
							$58.37	$57.88	$57.39	$56.90	$56.41	$55.91	$55.41
						$47.84	$47.36	$46.87	$46.38	$45.89	$45.40	$44.90	$44.40
					$38.14	$37.64	$37.14	$36.64	$36.15	$35.66	$35.17	$34.67	$34.17
				$29.34	$28.80	$28.26	$27.72	$27.19	$26.66	$26.15	$25.66	$25.16	$24.66
			$21.63	$21.04	$20.45	$19.85	$19.24	$18.62	$18.01	$17.40	$16.83	$16.33	$15.83
		$15.21	$14.61	$13.99	$13.36	$12.70	$12.02	$11.32	$10.58	$9.80	$8.98	$8.12	$7.63
	$10.18	$9.62	$9.04	$8.44	$7.82	$7.18	$6.51	$5.80	$5.04	$4.21	$3.26	$2.09	$0.00
		$5.52	$5.02	$4.51	$3.99	$3.46	$2.91	$2.35	$1.77	$1.18	$0.57	$0.00	$0.00
			$2.45	$2.08	$1.72	$1.36	$1.02	$0.70	$0.40	$0.16	$0.00	$0.00	$0.00
				$0.81	$0.60	$0.42	$0.26	$0.13	$0.04	$0.00	$0.00	$0.00	$0.00
					$0.16	$0.09	$0.04	$0.01	$0.00	$0.00	$0.00	$0.00	$0.00
						$0.01	$0.00	$0.00	$0.00	$0.00	$0.00	$0.00	$0.00
							$0.00	$0.00	$0.00	$0.00	$0.00	$0.00	$0.00
								$0.00	$0.00	$0.00	$0.00	$0.00	$0.00
									$0.00	$0.00	$0.00	$0.00	$0.00
										$0.00	$0.00	$0.00	$0.00
											$0.00	$0.00	$0.00
												$0.00	$0.00
													$0.00

FIGURE 12.25

Hull White Model

$$U = e^{\sigma\sqrt{3t}} \quad d = 1/u$$

$$Pu = \sqrt{\frac{t}{12\sigma^2}}\,(r - .5\sigma^2) + \frac{1}{6}$$

$$Pd = -\sqrt{\frac{t}{12\sigma^2}}\,(r - .5\sigma^2) + \frac{1}{6}$$

$$Pm = 2/3$$

$U = e^{\sigma\sqrt{3t}}$

$D = 1/u$

$P_u = \sqrt{t/12\sigma^2}\,(r - .5\sigma^2) + 1/6$

$P_d = \sqrt{t/12\sigma^2}\,(r - .5\sigma^2) + 1/6$

$P_m = 2/3$

												1
											1	12
										1	11	78
									1	10	66	352
								1	9	55	275	1,221
							1	8	45	210	880	3,432
						1	7	36	156	615	2,277	8,074
					1	6	28	112	414	1,452	4,917	16,236
				1	5	21	77	266	882	2,850	9,042	28,314
			1	4	15	50	161	504	1,554	4,740	14,355	43,252
		1	3	10	30	90	266	784	2,304	6,765	19,855	58,278
	1	2	6	16	45	126	357	1,016	2,907	8,350	24,068	69,576
1	1	3	7	19	51	141	393	1,107	3,139	8,953	25,653	73,789
	1	2	6	16	45	126	357	1,016	2,907	8,350	24,068	69,576
		1	3	10	30	90	266	784	2,304	6,765	19,855	58,278
			1	4	15	50	161	504	1,554	4,740	14,355	43,252
				1	5	21	77	266	882	2,850	9,042	28,314
					1	6	28	112	414	1,452	4,917	16,236
						1	7	36	156	615	2,277	8,074
							1	8	45	210	880	3,432
								1	9	55	275	1,221
									1	10	66	352
										1	11	78
											1	12
												1

												.0000%
											.0001%	.0004%
										.0003%	.0014%	.0043%
									.0009%	.0046%	.0131%	.0287%
								.0033%	.0149%	.0392%	.0792%	.1364%
							.01%	.0481%	.1146%	.2129%	.3407%	.4937%
						.04%	.15%	.3262%	.5532%	.8192%	1.1104%	1.4153%
					.16%	.47%	.90%	1.3782%	1.8780%	2.3730%	2.8479%	3.2944%
				.58%	1.44%	2.36%	3.25%	4.0546%	4.7602%	5.3702%	5.8926%	6.3372%
			2.09%	4.17%	5.85%	7.13%	8.09%	8.8088%	9.3362%	9.7225%	10.0015%	10.1985%
		7.59%	11.36%	13.22%	14.12%	14.53%	14.66%	14.6191%	14.4882%	14.3018%	14.0835%	13.8480%
	27.55%	27.48%	25.70%	23.93%	22.38%	21.05%	19.90%	18.9051%	18.0333%	17.2619%	16.5735%	15.9544%
100.00%	49.88%	37.31%	31.02%	27.07%	24.31%	22.23%	20.59%	19.2527%	18.1381%	17.1886%	16.3667%	15.6459%
	22.57%	22.52%	21.06%	19.61%	18.34%	17.25%	16.31%	15.4917%	14.7772%	14.1451%	13.5810%	13.0737%
		5.10%	7.63%	8.87%	9.48%	9.76%	9.84%	9.8165%	9.7286%	9.6034%	9.4568%	9.2987%
			1.15%	2.30%	3.22%	3.93%	4.45%	4.8470%	5.1372%	5.3497%	5.5033%	5.6116%
				.26%	.65%	1.07%	1.47%	1.8282%	2.1463%	2.4214%	2.6569%	2.8574%
					.06%	.18%	.33%	.5092%	.6939%	.8768%	1.0522%	1.2172%
						.01%	.05%	.0988%	.1675%	.2480%	.3362%	.4285%
							.00%	.0119%	.0284%	.0528%	.0845%	.1225%
								.0007%	.0030%	.0080%	.0161%	.0277%
									.0002%	.0008%	.0022%	.0048%
										.0000%	.0002%	.0006%
											.0000%	.0000%
												.0000%

BLACK SCHOLES

As the time increments between the binomial or trinomial steps become smaller, more data points are available at the terminal value. If the time steps become infinitely small, the solutions for call and put pricing become the integral equation known as Black Scholes (see Figure 12.26). Figures 12.27 through 12.29 depict the use of Black Scholes on underlyings that pay a continuous rate, on futures, and on FX rates, respectively.

FIGURE 12.26

Black Scholes Option Pricing Formula

$$d_1 = \frac{\ln\left[\frac{MV}{K}\right] + \left[r + \frac{\sigma^2}{2}\right]t}{\sigma\sqrt{t}}$$

$$d_2 = d_1 - \sigma\sqrt{t}$$

$$\text{Call} = MV \times N(d_1) - Ke^{-rt} \times N(d_2)$$

$$\text{Put} = -N(-d_1) \times MV + Ke^{-rt} \times N(-d_2)$$

As an example:

Market value = 100
Dividends = $0.00
Strike price = 100
d_1 = .78262
Volatility = 30%
d_2 = .11180
Interest rate = 6%
Call = $37.97
Time frame = 5
Put = $12.05

Notes:

- N stands for the standard normal distribution function—
  NORM.S.DIST() in Excel.

- For interest calculations, use 360 or actual days—depending on how rate is quoted.
- For trading days, use 250, 252, or 290—depending upon the number of trading days in the market.
- Subtract the PV of any dividends; discount from the ex-date, not payment date.
- Payment of dividends increases short-term volatility—reduces long-term volatility.
- Build in expected dividend changes.
- In case of index, convert dividend yield to a continuous rate (q below).

FIGURE 12.27

Black Scholes When Underlying Pays a Continuous Rate

$$d_1 = \frac{\ln\left[\dfrac{MV}{K}\right] + \left[(r - q) + \dfrac{\sigma^2}{2}\right]t}{\sigma\sqrt{t}}$$

$$d_2 = d_1 - \sigma\sqrt{t}$$

$$\text{Call} = MV \times N(d_1)e^{-qt} - Ke^{-rt} \times N(d_2)$$

$$\text{Put} = Ke^{-rt} \times N(-d_2) - MVe^{-qt} \times N(-d_1)$$

FIGURE 12.28

Pricing Options on Futures

$$d_1 = \frac{\ln\left[\dfrac{F}{K}\right] + \left[\dfrac{\sigma^2}{2}\right]t}{\sigma\sqrt{t}}$$

$$d_2 = d_1 - \sigma\sqrt{t}$$

$$\text{Call} = e^{-qt}\left[FN(d_1) - K(d_2)\right]$$

$$\text{Put} = e^{-qt}\left[KN(-d_2) - FN(-d_1)\right]$$

EXAMPLE: OPTION ON PALLADIUM FORWARD

Price underling: $950 spot price

Forward price = $1,000

Strike = $1,050

Volatility = 30%

Rate = 8% cc A/360

$$d_1 = \frac{\ln\left[\dfrac{\$1,000}{\$1,050}\right] + \left[\dfrac{.3^2}{2}\right]5}{.3\sqrt{5}} = .64628786$$

$$d_2 = d_1 - \sigma\sqrt{t} = -0.147503248$$

$$\text{Call} = e^{-.08(.5)}\left[\$1,000N(d_1) - \$1,050(d_2)\right] = \$77.34$$

$$\text{Put} = e^{-.08(.5)}\left[\$1,050N(-d_2) - \$1,000N(-d_1)\right] = \$85.83$$

FIGURE 12.29

Options on FX Rates

$$d_1 = \frac{\ln\left[\dfrac{FXrate}{K}\right] + \left[r_{domestic} - r_{domestic} + \dfrac{\sigma^2}{2}\right]t}{\sigma\sqrt{t}}$$

$$d_2 = d_1 - \sigma\sqrt{t}$$

$$Call = FXe^{-rft}N(d_1) - Ke^{rdt}(d_2)$$

$$Put = Ke^{-rdt}N(-d_2) - FXe^{-rft}N(-d_1)$$

EXAMPLE: CALL ON POUNDS/PUT ON DOLLARS

GBP/USD = $1.56

Strike = $1.60

Dollar rate = 6% cc 30/360

Pound rate = 8% cc 30/360

Volatility = 12%

$$d_1 = \frac{\ln\left[\dfrac{1.56}{1.60}\right] + \left[.06 - .08 + \dfrac{.12^2}{2}\right].5}{.12\sqrt{.5}} = -0.3738$$

$$d_2 = d_1 - \sigma\sqrt{t} = -4587$$

$$\text{Call} = 1.56^{-.08(.5)}\,N(d_1) - 1.60e^{-.06(.5)}\,N(d_2) = .0291$$

$$\text{Put} = 1.60e^{-.06(.5)}\,N(-d_2) - 1.56e^{-.08(.5)}\,N(-d_1) = .0830$$

CHAPTER THIRTEEN

Option Sensitivities

In the last chapter, regardless of which model was used for pricing, the inputs were the same:

- Risk-free rate
- Strike price
- Market value
- Time to expiration
- Volatility assumption

The strike price generally is fixed. The option sensitivities measure how the value of the option changes when one of the other inputs changes.

DELTA

An option's delta measures the change in the option's price in response to a change in market value. Using the raffle ticket analogy

developed in the chapter on pricing, consider the lognormal distribution of prices versus the various strike prices, as shown in Figure
13.1. This is the estimated distribution of the underlying's price in
1 year.

FIGURE 13.1

Alternative Strike Prices

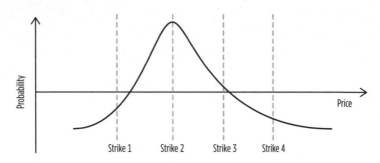

Assume strike 2 is at the current spot price. As of this moment,
the probabilities that each 1-year call option will be in the money
is equal to the area to the right of the strike relative to the total area
under the curve. Thus the probability that the 1-year calls will be
in the money is as shown in Figure 13.2.

FIGURE 13.2

Probability of Strike Prices Being in the Money

	Strike 1	Strike 2	Strike 3	Strike 4
Call Options	ITM	ATM	OTM	OTM
Probability of ITM	87%	60%	24%	4%

Consider strike 1: As of now, there is an 87% chance that the
option will end up in the money. If the price of the underlying rises
by $1.00, there is:

- An 87% chance the option will end up in the money and the long will profit by $1.00.
- A 13% chance the option will end up out of the money and the long will benefit by $0.00.

An 87% chance of winning $1.00 a year from today is the PV of $0.87, as follows:

= Present value (win × probability of win)
= Present value ($1.00 × .87)

Assuming a 5% rate:

= $0.87 / (1.05) = $0.83

Thus, a $1.00 rise in the value of the underlying should result in a $0.83 change in the value of the option with the first strike. Therefore, this option's delta is .83. Naturally, a $1.00 decline in the value of the underlying would cause the option's value to drop by $0.83.

Following the same logic, the delta of the other three calls is:

- Strike 2 = $0.60 / 1.05 = $0.57
- Strike 3 = $0.24 / 1.05 = $0.23
- Strike 4 = $0.04 / 1.05 = $0.04

The delta for call options ranges from:

- "0" for options that currently are so far out of the money that the probability of them being in the money at expiration is 0%
- "1" for options that currently are so far in the money that the probability of then being in the money at expiration is virtually 100%.

FIGURE 13.3

Probability of Puts Being in the Money

	Strike 1	Strike 2	Strike 3	Strike 4
Put Options	OTM	ATM	ITM	ITM
Probability of ITM	13%	40%	76%	96%

In the case of puts, the probability of being in the money is the opposite of the calls. Thus, the put at strike 1 has a 13% chance of being in the money at expiration, while the call's probability is 87%. Likewise, the put at strike 4 has a 96% chance of being in the money, while the call had a 4% chance.

Delta is always quoted as the change in the option's value in response to a $1.00 gain in the underlying's value, so the delta of puts is negative and ranges from –1 to 0. For these four strikes, the deltas are:

–$0.13 / 1.05 = –$0.12

–$0.40 / 1.05 = –$0.38

–$0.76 / 1.05 = –$0.72

–$0.96 / 1.05 = –$0.91

Applications of Delta

Delta has three main applications: relative value analysis, leverage analysis, and delta neutral hedging.

> **Relative value analysis**—Suppose that an investor is debating between buying either:
> - 25,000 shares of IBM @ $200 each for a cost of $5MM
> - Long-dated listed ATM call options currently selling at $1,000 per contract

When comparing the two alternatives, the relative value analysis should not be performed between the stock and 250 option contacts. The two positions are not equal. If the ATM calls have a delta of .6, when the stock rises by $1.00, the option price will only change by $0.60. Thus, a $1.00 increase in the value of the stock causes a $25,000 increase in the value of the stock position, but only a $15,000 (25,000 shares × $1.00 × .6) increase in the value of the options.

A fair relative value analysis would require that both positions have equal volatility. In this example:

> 25,000 shares of stock / .6 = 41,666 options or 417 option contracts

Thus, the choice between two equal positions with equal volatility is $5MM of stock vs. $417 × 1,000 = 417,000 worth of options.

Leverage analysis—In the scenario we considered for relative value analysis, buying the option instead of the stock does not provide 20 times leverage ($200 stock / $10 option), as many investors assume. Because the option has less volatility, it takes $10/.6 = $16.67 worth of options to have equal volatility. The actual leverage from a notionally equal (1 share vs. 1 option) analysis is $200 / $16.67 = 12 times leverage.

Delta neutral hedging—An investor owns 100,000 ounces of gold and the spot price is $2,000 an ounce. The investor wants to hedge the risk of holding the gold using ATM 6-month puts. How many puts are required to hedge the risk assuming a delta of -.45? At first glance, it would appear that 100,000 options (1,000 contracts) is the answer and it *may* be the right answer if the investor is *only* worried about being hedged on the option's expiration date. In 6 months, if gold is below $2,000, the long would use the options to liquidate the position at $2,000 per ounce.

If, however, the investor wants to be hedged *over* the time frame from today until 6 months from now, the 1,000-contracts hedge won't work. If tomorrow, gold were to decline by $1 an ounce, the gold position would be down $100,000, but the option position would only be up by $45,000—for a net loss at the end of the day of $55,000. While this will balance out by maturity of the put, on a day-to-day basis, the positions will not hedge each other.

To be hedged from today until tomorrow requires a delta neutral hedge. A delta neutral hedge is one with equal volatilities on both sides. In this case, 100,000 ounces / .45 delta = 222,222. Due to the factors discussed in the next section, the delta is constantly changing, so the hedge must be rebalanced periodically. As a general rule, dealers use delta neutral positions to hedge their positions overnight. Investors use positions that are notionally equal and only hedge the risk at expiration.

Factors That Impact Delta

The three factors that impact delta are volatility, time to expiration, and the change in market value.

If volatility decreases, the lognormal curve becomes steeper and narrower, causing the probability that options will be in the money at expiration to change. Specifically, the delta of in-the-money options increases and out of the money decreases, as shown in Figure 13.4. The passage of time causes the same change. (See Figure 13.5, Figure 13.6, and Figure 13.7.)

FIGURE 13.4

Impact of Changing Volatility on Delta

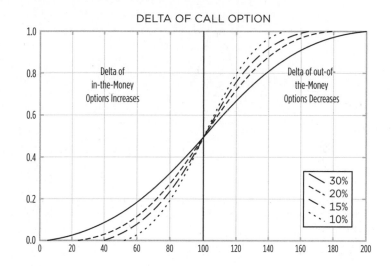

FIGURE 13.5

Impact of the Passage of Time

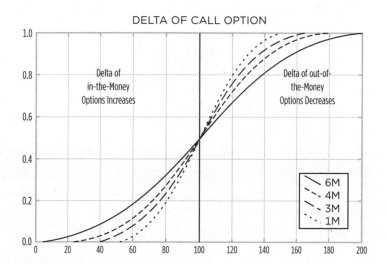

FIGURE 13.6

As Time Passes, the Curve Narrows and Steepens

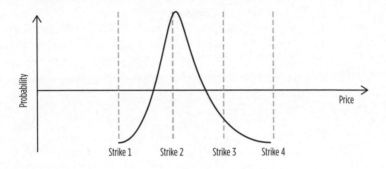

FIGURE 13.7

Result of Time Passages

	Strike 1	Strike 2	Strike 3	Strike 4
Call Options	ITM	ATM	OTM	OTM
Probability of ITM	100%	60%	15%	0%
	Strike 1	**Strike 2**	**Strike 3**	**Strike 4**
Put Options	OTM	ATM	ITM	ITM
Probability of ITM	0%	40%	85%	100%

GAMMA

As the MV of the underlying changes, the delta of the options also changes. The delta changes because, as the MV changes, the entire curve shifts to the right or left. In the example shown in Figure 13.8, the curve shifts to the right, and the probability of the various strike prices being in the money changes.

FIGURE 13.8

Shift of Curve as Price Changes

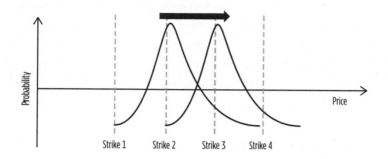

FIGURE 13.9

Change in the Probability of Being in the Money

	Strike 1	Strike 2	Strike 3	Strike 4
Call Options	ITM	ATM	OTM	OTM
Probability of ITM Before Shift	100%	60%	15%	0%
Probability of ITM After Shift	100%	100%	60%	15%

Gamma measures the change in the delta due to a change in the market value and, therefore, is the second derivative of the change in market value. Since the delta changes as the market value changes, the total price change in the value of the option is:

PV[existing delta ± gamma from price move]

Gamma is the primary advantage that the longs enjoy— especially those who are long options that have out-of-the-money strikes. Consider being long the strike 3 call before the price moves. If we assume that there is an equal probability of an equally sized up move and a down move in the price of the underlying over the short term, then there is an unequal-size increase and decrease in the value of the option.

Consider the information in Figure 13.10: Initially, there is a 24% chance that a call with strike 3 will be in the money. If the price rises by $5, the probability of being in the money increases to 35%—up 9%. If the price declines by $5, the probability of being in the money declines to 18%—down 6%.

FIGURE 13.10

Uneven Gamma for Equal Moves

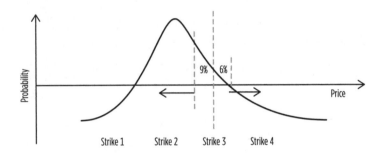

When the curve shifts to the right, the slice of the curve that gets added becomes larger than the size of the slice that is subtracted when the curve shifts to the left.

Price change up = PV[24% delta + 9% gamma] = 33% gain
Price change down = PV[24% delta − 6% gamma] = 18% loss

Gamma increases as the time to expiration decreases because the price curve becomes steeper and narrower. Therefore, the height of each slice of the curve becomes larger.

THETA

Theta is the impact of a passage of time on the price of an option. As time passes, the distribution of future prices becomes steeper and narrower. The value of options declines with the passage of time.

- The value of far out-of-the-money options declines at a fairly stable rate. Their value is all time value.
- The value of far in-the-money options also declines at a fairly stable rate. The deeper they are in the money, the less leverage they offer.
- The value of at-the-money options remains stable the longest—but then loses value very quickly as the option approaches maturity. The gamma of ATM options is very high.

Several option strategies depend upon the differential in rates at which options lose their time value as time passes.

Theta is the primary advantage of being short on options. Every day that passes lowers the value of an option—all other factors remaining equal.

VEGA

Vega is the sensitivity to changes in volatility. As the volatility of the underlying increases, the distribution curve becomes wider and flatter, increasing the potential win for all options. As volatility declines, the value of all options on the underlying declines.

CHAPTER FOURTEEN

Volatility

Volatility is a statistical measure of the degree to which the underlying's instruments' daily price movements deviate from the central tendency of its daily price movements. It is one of five inputs used by most option pricing models to determine the theoretical value of an option. In fact, since the other four inputs are directly observable, option pros often trade options based on volatility instead of price. If you know the volatility of the underlying, you know the theoretical price of the option. If you know the theoretical price of the option, you know the historic volatility of the underlying. The relationship is directly analogous to a bond's yield and price. If you know one, you can calculate the other.

Volatility is not caused by more buyers than sellers or more sellers than buyers. It is caused by more aggressive buyers or more aggressive sellers, each of whom have different investment horizons, price goals, risk tolerances, constraints, and alternative opportunities. Collectively their actions create price changes that appear to be random, as shown in Figure 14.1. (The CF in the equation is the confidence factor.)

FIGURE 14.1

The Formula for Calculating Volatility

$$\sigma = \sqrt{\left\{ \frac{\left[\sum_{1}^{n}\left[\left(\ln\left(\frac{S_T}{S_{T-1}}\right)\right)^2\right]\right]}{n-1} \right\} - \left\{ \frac{\left[\sum_{1}^{n}\ln\left(\frac{S_T}{S_{T-1}}\right)\right]^2}{n \times (n-1)} \right\}} \quad \sqrt{\text{Trading Days}} \times CF$$

CF 1.28=90%
CF 1.64=95%
CF 2.33=99%

In effect, you are calculating the daily price change and comparing it to the average price change. The number of trading days is usually considered to be 252 in the United States, although round-the-clock trading is changing this.

Whenever a subset of data is used to calculate volatility, there is always a chance that the subset has less volatility than the entire population. Therefore, the volatility of the subset is multiplied by a CF to increase the odds that the volatility of the population is greater than the subset. For example, multiplying the volatility of the subset by 1.28 increases the odds that the population's volatility is not higher than 90%.

FIGURE 14.2

Example Calculation of Volatility

Day #	Value of Stock	Price Relative	Daily Return	Daily Squared Return
0	$100.00			
1	$100.10	1.00100000	.0009995	.0000009990
2	$99.80	.99700000	-.003004509	.0000090271
3	$100.60	1.00800000	.00796817	.0000634917
4	$100.40	.99800000	-.002002003	.0000040080
5	$99.69	.99300000	-.007024615	.0000493452
6	$100.39	1.00700000	.006975614	.0000486592
7	$101.50	1.01100000	.01093994	.0001196823
8	$102.11	1.00600000	.005982072	.0000357852
9	$100.37	.98300000	-.017146159	.0002939908
10	$98.66	.98300000	-.017146159	.0002939908
11	$97.38	.98700000	-.01308524	.0001712235
12	$96.70	.99300000	-.007024615	.0000493452
13	$97.86	1.01200000	.011928571	.0001422908
14	$97.76	.99900000	-.0010005	.0000010010
15	$98.54	1.00800000	.00796817	.0000634917
16	$96.77	.98200000	-.018163971	.0003299298
17	$95.90	.99100000	-.009040745	.0000817351

Day #	Value of Stock	Price Relative	Daily Return	Daily Squared Return
18	$97.91	1.02100000	.020782539	.0004319139
19	$99.97	1.02100000	.020782539	.0004319139
20	$101.47	1.01500000	.014888612	.0002216708
21	$103.40	1.01900000	.018821754	.0003542584
22	$104.84	1.01400000	.013902905	.0001932908
23	$106.00	1.01100000	.01093994	.0001196823
24	$104.83	.98900000	−.011060947	.0001223446
25	$106.40	1.01500000	.014888612	.0002216708
26	$107.15	1.00700000	.006975614	.0000486592
27	$108.54	1.01300000	.012916225	.0001668289
28	$107.46	.99000000	−.010050336	.0001010093
29	$107.89	1.00400000	.003992021	.0000159362
30	$109.07	1.01100000	.01093994	.0001196823
		Sum	.086842941	.0043068577
		Sum Square	.007541696	
		Divided 1/(30 × 29)	.00000867	.0001485123
		S =	.011825554	
		252 days	.187724843	
		Confidence factor	24.03%	

In the calculation shown in Figure 14.2, it's not really the stock's volatility that's being measured—that's a misnomer. Instead, it's the *change* in the volatility of the stock's price that is being measured. As such:

- The initial price is irrelevant when calculating volatility.
- It makes no difference if the price move is up or down.
- If the stock price stays flat, there is no volatility.

- If the stock price changes by the same percentage, there is no volatility.
- If the stock price changes by the same amount, there is volatility since each change is proportionally smaller as the price rises.
- Equal volatilities don't mean equal price patterns; one stock can have consistent smaller moves while others have fewer large moves, and both can have the same volatility.
- Volatility of an underlying can change over time. For example, the S&P 500 has had a volatility as low as 10% and as high as 100%.
- Volatility has its own volatility, which complicates option pricing.
- The volatility of a future depends upon the volatility of the spot, the volatility of the cost of carry, and the correlation of the two.
- Volatility is auto-correlating; high-volatility days tend to be followed by high-volatility days, and low-volatility days are followed by low-volatility days.

There are three types of volatility: historic, implied, and realized:

Historic volatility—Historic volatility is the past volatility of the underlying. Most option pricing models assume that the underlying's past volatility is indicative of its future volatility, as shown in Figure 14.3. The historic volatility is very dependent upon the amount of data used in the calculation—30 days, 60 days, 90 days, and so on—and how the data is weighted (linear or exponential).

FIGURE 14.3

Options Pricing Model

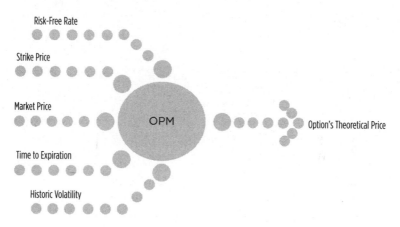

Implied volatility—Implied volatility is the volatility that's *implied* by the price of the option in the market. By starting with the option's market price and working backward through the option pricing model, it is possible to calculate the volatility implied by the market's price, as shown in Figure 14.4. Investors and traders look for underlying instruments where there is a divergence between the underlying instrument's historic and implied volatility. When there is a significant divergence between the historic and implied volatility, the option is either mispriced—or there is something going on at the company. This becomes a key to determining the appropriate option strategy. We'll discuss option strategies in the next chapter.

FIGURE 14.4

Implied Volatility Model

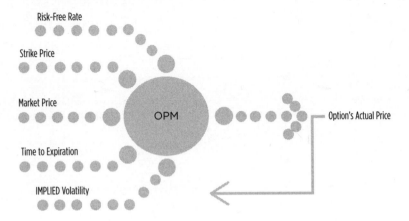

Realized volatility—The realized volatility is the actual volatility over a time frame. It can only be determined after the fact.

CHAPTER FIFTEEN

Option Strategies

Investors considering IBM stock only have to have an outlook on the future price of the stock:

- They go long if the stock is expected to rise (possibly on margin) and if they want to be aggressive.
- They ignore it if the stock is expected to stay flat.
- They go short if the is expected to decline and always on margin.

However, investors considering IBM options not only need an outlook on the direction of the stock's price; they also need an outlook on the magnitude of the movement and on the time frame over which the move will occur. The investor also needs to determine how confident they are with regard to their assessment of direction, magnitude, and time frame. (See Figure 15.1.)

FIGURE 15.1

Issues That Impact Option Strategy Selection

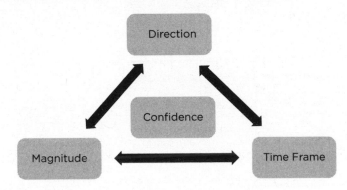

Suppose an investor is bullish on IBM common when it is selling at $200. The investor has $50,000 to invest and has to decide on an expiration date, strike price, whether to go long calls, short puts, or to use a position that requires multiple option positions. Let's start with the strategies that utilize calls, as shown in Figure 15.2.

FIGURE 15.2

Call Prices

Strike	3 months	6 months	9 months	12 months
$300	NA	$0.01	$0.02	$0.04
$280	$0.01	$0.05	$0.10	$0.13
$260	$0.10	$0.25	$0.40	$0.50
$240	$2.00	$5.50	$7.00	$8.00
$220	$8.00	$15.00	$21.00	$25.00
$200	$20.00	$26.00	$31.00	$35.00
$180	$35.00	$45.00	$50.00	$52.00

Expiration Date

The investor believes the stock will rise from $200 to $260 in 6 months. The most obvious strategy is to look at the call options that expire in 6 months.

Assuming the investor is right about direction, price, and magnitude, if the investor buys the ATM calls, the profit at expiration will be as depicted in Figure 15.3.

FIGURE 15.3

Alternative Possibilities

Strike	Premium	# of Options	Breakeven	Payoff	Intrinsic	Profit
$260	$0.25	200,000	$260.25	$0	$0	−$50,000
$240	$5.50	9,091	$245.50	$14.50	$131,818.18	$81,818.18
$220	$15.00	3,333	$235.00	$25.00	$83,333.33	$33,333,33
$200	$26.00	1,923	$226.00	$34.00	$65,384.62	$15,384.62

At first glance, it appears the $240 calls would be the best choice, however:

- Suppose that the investor is overly optimistic about the magnitude of the move, and the stock is at $239 in 6 months. In this case, the $220 strike would be a much better choice.
- Suppose that the investor is wrong about the timing, and the stock moves either faster or slower than expected. In this case, the 3-month or 9-month might be a better deal.
- Suppose that the investor is overly conservative about the magnitude of the move, and the stock ends at $265 instead of $260. Buying the $260s would then offer a profit of $950,000 at expiration instead of a $50,000 loss. Of course, the options don't have to be held until expiration. If the price

approaches $265 before expiration, the $260 calls can be sold before maturity for a huge profit even if they are worthless at expiration.

- The investor could also sell the $220s and use the premium received to buy the additional $200s. This can increase return without increasing magnitude risk.
- The investor could also sell the $260 puts (up to the margin limit) then simply keep the premium (approximately $63 per option) and hope they expire worthless.

The right approach depends upon how confident the investor is with regard to the outlook for direction, magnitude, and timing. In addition to the outlooks, before an investor implements a strategy, an intelligent investor should know the following:

- Positions that have been taken to implement the strategy
- Maximum profit and loss
- Break-even point(s)
- Equivalent positions, if any
- Sensitivities (delta, gamma, theta, vega)
- The point where you declare success and close out the trade
- The point where you admit failure and close out the trade

The most common option strategies fall into two categories: direction and volatility. While every strategy has an exposure to both, direction strategies are mainly bets on whether the price of the underlying will move up or down. Volatility strategies, on the other hand, are mainly bets on whether volatility will increase or decrease. Figure 15.4 lists alternative strategies.

FIGURE 15.4

Alternative Strategies

Direction	Volatility
Long calls	Calendar spread
Short calls	Reverse calendar spread
Long puts	Long straddle
Short puts	Long strangle
Covered call writing	Short straddle
Covered put writing	Short strangle
Bull call spread	Long iron butterfly
Bull put spread	Short iron butterfly
Bear call spread	Delta neutral call writes
Bear put spread	Delta neutral put writes

Let's look at some mini case studies (HV is historic volatility; IV is implied volatility):

Case 1—XYZ is selling at $80 a share. You don't own the stock but believe that the stock will rise to $120 over the next 6 months. The HV is 34%, the IV is 22%. What strategy would you implement?

Since the option's IV < HV the options are cheap. Therefore, it makes sense to buy options instead of buying the underlying or selling options. You can buy the ATM 80 calls, the 85 calls, the 90 calls, and so on.

Suppose your degree of confidence that the stock would move from $80 to $120 was very high—how would that impact your strategy, if at all?

The higher the investor's degree of confidence, the higher the strike price, and the higher the leverage.

Case 2—XYZ is selling at $80 a share. You don't own the stock but believe that the stock will rise to $120 over the next 6 months. The HV is 22%, the IV is 34%. What strategy would you implement?

In this case the options are expensive, so it makes more sense to buy the underlying instrument or sell puts instead of buying calls. The higher the investor's degree of confidence, the more attractive it is to sell puts and the higher the strike price at which they sell them.

Case 3—XYZ is currently selling at $70. You believe it is fully priced. You are a broker and you call a client who bought the stock at $40 and suggest he sell the stock. The client says that he thinks the stock has another 10 points of upside left in it. The stock's HV is 20% and the option's IV is 30%. What option strategy, if any, would you recommend?

The client is unwilling to sell at $70 but has disclosed a target of $80. Suggest selling the $80 call (let's assume for $2.50) and putting in a stop-loss order at $67.50. If the client follows your advice, there are three possibilities. The price:

- Rises above $80 and the stock is called away. The client was going to sell at $80 anyway, and the net sales proceeds are really $82.50.
- Falls, in which case the stock is sold at $67.50—or net $70 when you count the $2.50 option premium, which expires worthless.
- Stays between $70 and $80, in which case the $2.50 provides nice income.

Case 4—You are a broker. Over the past 6 months, XYZ Inc. has moved from $40 to $70 a share. The IV is 34%, the HV is 32%, and your firm's research department has a target price of $80 a share. The client currently doesn't own the stock. What option strategy, if any, would you recommend?

In this case the options are fairly priced—a 2% difference between HV and IV being meaningless. You could:

- *Buy the stock.* This uses a lot of capital, has a $10 upside (to your target of $80), and has a $30 downside. If the stock can go from $40 to $70, it can go from $70 to $40.
- *Buy the $70 call.* This option will probably cost $6–$7. If the research department is correct and the stock rises to $80, the investor makes $3–$4. Risking $6–$7 to make $3–$4 is not attractive.
- *Buy the $70 call and sell the $80 call.* The net cash outlay drops to $3–$4 and the gain rises to $6–$7. This is known as a bull call spread.

Spreads are usually the solution when the expected price move in the underlying is relatively small.

Case 5—You are a broker. You call a client and suggest she buy XYZ Inc. when it is selling for $80 a share. The client says she likes the stock long term, but thinks it might trade down over the short term to $70. The IV is 20%. The HV is 18%. What strategy would you recommend?

Since the client has indicated she's a buyer at $70, let's get her paid for making that decision. She can get paid by selling the $70 put. If she sells the $70 put for $2.00, three things can happen. The price of XYZ:

- Rises and the client misses the move, but at least she collected $2.00 per share.
- Declines and the client gets the stock at $70. She was going to buy it at $70 anyway and, considering the $2.00 option premium, her net cost is $68.
- Stays flat, in which case at least the client collects $2.00.

Case 6—XYZ is selling at $80 a share. You don't own the stock but believe that the stock will rise to $110, but not for 6 months or so. The HV is 34%; the IV is 45%. What strategy do you implement? In this case, you might want to sell the:

- 3-month 90 calls and the 70 puts
- 6-month 95 calls and the 75 puts (the strike price is a little higher in case the stock starts to move ahead of schedule)

Figure 15.5 provides a visual representation of the strategy.

FIGURE 15.5

Strategy Based on Outlook for Prices

Today	3 Months	6 Months	9 Months	12 Months
				$120
	Sell $90 call	Sell $95 call	$100	Buy $80 call
$80 →	$80 →	$80 →		
	Sell $70 put	Sell $75 put		

You hope that the 3-month and 6-month options all expire worthless. The proceeds from these option sales can be used to buy 12-month calls. Whether it makes sense to buy the calls with the $80, $85, $90, $95, $100, $105, or $110 strike depends on the investor's level of confidence.

Case 7—XYZ Inc. has moved from $60 to $70 in some anticipation of a takeover. Your client does not think the takeover will go through, but wants to profit regardless of whether it does or not. What strategy would you recommend?

In this case, the stock has drifted up on the rumor of a takeover. If the company is the subject of a takeover attempt, you expect it will be at $85. If the first bid starts a takeover war, the price could go as high as $95. If the takeover falls apart, the disappointment could cause the stock to drop from $70 to $50.

You have no way of handicapping whether the takeover will occur, so you want a strategy that will profit regardless. One way to do that would be to buy the $70 call and the $70 put. Obviously, one or the other will expire worthless, but you hope that the profit on the other exceeds the cost of both.

CHAPTER SIXTEEN

Exotic Options

An exotic option is an option that differs from a traditional option in one (or more) of three ways; it offers investors a different:

- Probability of winning
- Magnitude of the win
- Timing of the premium payment and/or the settlement payoff

Each change results in the option having a different price, break-even, and risk-reward profile than a traditional option. Exotic options offer several possible advantages over traditional options. They can allow investors to:

- Isolate the payoff so that it is exclusively a function of either the underlying's volatility or direction. The payoff of regular options is a function of both.
- Hedge or speculate on additional outlooks, such as "whether the correlation of two assets will increase or decrease." The

payoff of regular options is tied to the absolute performance of a single asset instead of the relative performance of multiple assets.

- Increase leverage without raising the strike price.
- Lower the cost of implementing an effective hedge.
- Increase the current income while holding (shorting) the underlying.
- Lower their transaction costs. Many exotics are composed of numerous options, which would be more expensive if purchased separately.
- Create precise solutions to typical business problems.
- Automate the implementation of various trading strategies.

Exotic options can be sorted into two categories: common exotic and customized exotic. Common exotics are well-known among investors and have readily accessible pricing models on investor platforms like Bloomberg. Some examples of common exotics:

- Asians
- Barriers
- Baskets
- Caps
- Choosers
- Compounds
- Contingent premium options
- Digitals
- Executive stock options
- Lookbacks
- Multiple-asset
- Quantos
- Spreads
- Step-up/Step-down

CONTINGENT PREMIUM OPTIONS

Contingent premium options, as the name implies, are options where the buyer might not have to pay for the option, depending upon the outcome of the position. Ask most investors, "How would you like an option that you only have to pay for if the option expires in the money?" And they'll say, "Sounds great." Of course, there is no free lunch. Consider the following contingent premium option:

Suppose a plain American 1-year 100-call option on XYZ is worth $10 when the stock is selling for $95. An investor wants an option that only has to be paid for if the option is in the money. If the option expires worthless, the investor never wants to pay for it. Pricing this option is fairly straightforward:

- Start by calculating the FV of the price of the plain option.
- Divide the FV by the probability that the option will be in the money at expiration.

If the option has a risk-free rate of 10% and the probability of being in the money at expiration is 50%, the premium would be:

$10 premium × 1.1 adjustment for time value of
money = $11 in a year / .50 = $22.00

From the seller's perspective the two approaches are economically equal:

- Selling the option today for $10 and investing the money for a year at 10% yields $11.00.

- Pricing the option in a year for $22—but only getting paid 50% of the time—yields $11.00.

The buyer of the option trades the chance of paying nothing if the option is out of the money for a breakeven of $122 ($100 strike plus $22.00 option) if it is in the money. Options that are paid for only if the option ends up in the money are referred to as Type-1 contingents.

Of course, this could be just as easily structured as an option that's only paid for if it ends up out of the money. These are Type-2 contingent options. Consider the following example:

Suppose a 6-month put on a bond with a strike price of $1,000 and a market value of $1,040 is $6.00. Assume that there is only a 15% chance that the option will be in the money at expiration, and the risk-free rate is 5%. In this case, the contingent put would be worth:

$$\$6.00 \times (1 + (.05 \times 180 / 360)) = \$6.15 / .85 = \$7.24$$

Since there is only an 85% chance the seller will get paid for the option, the premium has to be higher than the premium of a plain vanilla put.

There are also Type-3 contingent options. These are options that refund the premium if the option ends up in the money. Consider the following example:

Price of a plain vanilla call: $2

Term: 1 year

Risk-free rate: 8.00%

Strike: $100

Market value: $85

Probability option will be in the money: 12%

Probability of a refund: 12%

Value of probability weighted refund: 12% × $2 = $0.24

PV: $0.24 / 1.08 = $0.22

Premium with refund feature: $2.22

Any option (plain or exotic) can be turned into a Type-1, Type-2, or Type-3 contingent option.

Digital Options

Digital options have a set payoff if they are in the money. If the strike price of a digital call is $100, it doesn't matter if, at expiration, the underlying is $101 or $909; the payoff is the same. These are also referred to as bet options, binaries, or all-or-none options. The pricing is simple:

Pricing = PV[payoff specified in the contract ×
    probability of ITM]

Digital options are sometimes used to hedge large possible future payments. Suppose a newly hired CEO is promised a $10MM bonus if the stock price, which is currently at $30 a share, rises above $60 a share within 3 years. If the probability of this happening is estimated at 10% and interest rates are at 3% per year the price would be:

($10,000,000 × .1) / (1 + .03)^3 = $915,142

Thus, the company's board of directors could hedge a potential $10MM expense in 3 years for less than $1MM today. If this risk is hedged, then the board and manager will both be ecstatic if the goal is achieved. The manager receives $10MM and so is ecstatic. The board of directors is thrilled since the $10MM bonus cost less than a million off the bottom line. Of course, if the goal is not achieved, the option expires worthless, costing the company $915,412.

CORRIDOR OPTIONS

A corridor option allows two parties with different outlooks on volatility to invest based on their view. Suppose IBM common is selling at $200 a share and rates are at 8%. Investor A thinks its price will remain reasonably constant (±$15) over the next year, while investor B thinks the price will primarily be outside this range. Investor A sells investor B an option that pays $5 for every trading day the stock closes outside the range. In effect, a corridor is a collection of 1-day digital options.

The option is priced using the current or historic volatility. Using the current volatility, a "Monte Carlo" simulation is set up in which the stock hypothetically is allowed to trade randomly at the historic volatility, and we determine on average how many days the option is in the money. For example, let's assume it's 100 days. The value of the option would be:

$$= PV \text{ (for } \frac{1}{2} \text{ year) } [(\$5 \text{ per day} \times 100 \text{ days})]$$
$$= \$500 / (1.04) = \$480.77$$

The option is priced using the current volatility. As shown in Figure 16.2, if the volatility:

- Stays the same, the value B receives should equal the FV of the premium B paid for the option: $500
- Increases, B should receive more than the FV of what B paid for the option: > $500
- Decreases, B should receive less than what B paid for the option: < $500

FIGURE 16.1

Payoff for Corridor Options

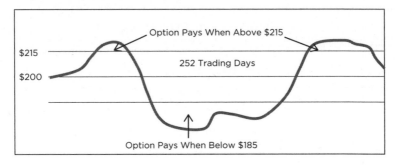

COMPOUND OPTIONS

A compound option is an option to buy or sell an option on an underlying:

- Ca-call is the right to buy a call on the underlying.
- Ca-put is the right to buy a put on the underlying.
- Pu-call is the right to sell a call on the underlying.
- Pu-put is the right to sell a put on the underlying.

Consider an example with the following specifications and a price tree, option tree, and ca-call tree as shown in Figure 16.2.

Underlying = $100

Strike = $100

Volatility = 20%

Expiration = 1 year

Steps = 6

Rate = 5.00%

FIGURE 16.2

The Price Tree, Option Tree, and the Ca-Call Tree

						$163.21
					$150.42	
				$138.62		$138.62
			$127.76		$127.76	
		$117.74		$117.74		$117.74
	$108.51		$108.51		$108.51	
$100.00		$100.00		$100.00		$100.00
	$92.16		$92.16		$92.16	
		$84.93		$84.93		$84.93
			$78.27		$78.27	
				$72.14		$72.14
					$66.48	
						$61.27

						$63.21
					$51.25	
				$40.28		$38.62
			$30.22		$28.59	
		$21.72		$19.39		$17.74
	$15.06		$12.49		$9.34	
$10.13		$7.78		$4.92		$0.00
	$4.73		$2.59		$0.00	
		$1.36		$0.00		$0.00
			$0.00		$0.00	
				$0.00		$0.00
					$0.00	
						$0.00

						$53.09
					$41.21	
				$30.32		$28.50
			$21.37		$18.54	
		$14.55		$11.63		$7.61
	$9.64		$7.10		$4.01	
$6.24		$4.25		$2.11		$0.00
	$2.51		$1.11		$0.00	
		$0.58		$0.00		$0.00
			$0.00		$0.00	
				$0.00		$0.00
					$0.00	
						$0.00

For $6.24, an investor could have the right to buy a call option at $10.13 that would, in turn, entitle the investor to buy the underlying for $100. The initial outlay is lower than a traditional option—but the breakeven is higher.

While compound options are primarily used to obtain leverage, they do have one business application. Suppose that:

- On February 15, a US company submits a fully binding bid to build a plant in the UK for £1,000MM when the GBP/USD = 1.5000. ("Fully binding" means that if the bid is accepted, the US company must build the plant—the company can't back out.)
- On June 15, the contract is awarded.

If the US company:

- Wins the bid in June, it has the risk that the dollar will strengthen against the pound—but this risk began in February. Suppose that between February and June the dollar strengthens to GBP/USD = 1.2000. Now, instead of receiving $1,500MM for the pounds paid on the contract, the US company will only receive $1,200MM. Thus, waiting until the contract is awarded to hedge the FX risk is too risky.

- Hedges the risk and locks in the GBP/USD = 1.5000 rate with back-to-back loans, a forward contract, or futures, it has FX risk, even if it doesn't win the contract. Suppose that in June the FX rate has changed to GBP/USD = 1.8000. At this point, the hedge has lost $300MM. If there is no contract, the company won't be receiving £1,000MM to generate an offsetting $300MM gain. Therefore, the company must eat the $300MM loss to close out its hedge. Thus, hedging the risk with anything other than an option is too risky.

- Hedges the risk with an option on an option, wins the contract, *and* if the dollar gets stronger, the company can use the option to lock in the rate of GBP/USD = 1.5000. However, if the dollar weakens, the company can lock in the now more favorable risk.

BARRIER OPTIONS

A barrier option is an option that is either activated (knocked-in) or deactivated (knocked-out) if the price of the underlying reaches the barrier price. They come in eight basic varieties and have a language all of their own. "Up" means the price has to move up to reach the barrier. "In" means the option is knocked-in when the barrier is reached. "Down" and "out" have the opposite meanings. The possible combinations are:

- Up-and-in call
- Down-and-in call
- Up-and-out call
- Down-and-out call

- Up-and-in put
- Down-and-in put
- Up-and-out put
- Down-and-out put

The barrier feature itself is extremely flexible and can have several characteristics:

Path dependent—For plain European options, only the strike and expiration value are relevant when determining the intrinsic value at expiration. Barrier options, however, are path dependent. The path the underlying follows though the price tree is an additional factor in determining the intrinsic value at expiration.

Inclusive or exclusive—If a barrier option is inclusive, a trade must occur *at* the barrier for the event (knock-in or knock-out) to be triggered. If the barrier is exclusive, the barrier must be crossed for the event to be triggered. Thus, in the case of a $20 up-and-in option, a trade at $20 will trigger an inclusive barrier—but a trade > $20 would be necessary to trigger an exclusive option. The barrier test can be performed:

- Anytime—a continuous or American barrier
- At expiration—a European barrier
- Only on certain dates—Bermudan barrier

Life of barrier—The barrier can exist for the entire life of the option or it can be a window barrier, in which the barrier only exists for part of the option's life.

- A partial window starts with the barrier feature on—and then at some point it is deactivated.

- A forward barrier starts with the barrier feature off—and then at some point it is activated.

Number of barriers—Most barrier options have a single barrier. Some have multiple barriers that must all be triggered—but can be triggered in any order. Some have multiple barriers that must all be triggered—and must also be triggered in a specific order:

Cross barriers—Triggering one barrier cancels another barrier(s).

James Bond barriers—Triggering one barrier creates another barrier(s).

Outside barriers—Barrier triggers an action on a different underlying than the option. For example, the barrier might be on the EUR/USD exchange rate, but the option could be on the right to buy oil.

Step-up (step-down) barriers—The barrier rises (falls) on a predetermined schedule over time.

Variable barriers—The barrier rises or falls over time tied to changes in an index or economic indicators.

Parisian barrier—The barrier has to be violated for more than X time (e.g., 5 days) continuously before it is triggered—this eliminates the triggering of an option from a "splash crash."

Parasian barrier—The barrier has to be violated for more than X time (e.g., 5 days) cumulatively before it is triggered.

PRICING A BARRIER OPTION

Barrier options are cheaper because paths through the tree that would otherwise be profitable are canceled—reducing the probability of success. For example, look at the price tree shown in Figure 16.3. If we assume a 50%/50% up move and down move, there are 64 possible paths through the tree, each of which has a 1/64th chance of occurring. Assume a 5% simple rate of interest.

Now, look at the forward tree shown in Figure 16.4. There are seven paths through the tree that would be valuable for a traditional put but that are not valuable for an up-and-out put with a strike at $100 and a barrier at $105. These seven paths have no value because, even though they ended up in the money, they were knocked out when the price went above $105.

FIGURE 16.3

Price Tree

						$136.00
					$130.00	
				$124.00		$126.00
			$118.00		$120.00	
		$112.00		$114.00		$116.00
	$106.00		$108.00		$110.00	
$100.00		$102.00		$104.00		$106.00
	$96.00		$98.00		$100.00	
		$92.00		$94.00		$96.00
			$88.00		$90.00	
				$84.00		$86.00
					$80.00	
						$76.00

FIGURE 16.4

Shaded Node Is Where the Path Is Canceled

1st Node	2nd Node	3rd Node	4th Node	5th Node	6th Node	7th Node	Payoff
$100	$106	$112	$108	$104	$100	$96	$4
$100	$106	$102	$108	$104	$100	$96	$4
$100	$106	$102	$98	$104	$100	$96	$4
$100	$106	$102	$98	$94	$100	$96	$4
$100	$106	$102	$98	$94	$90	$96	$4
$100	$106	$102	$98	$94	$90	$86	$14
$100	$96	$102	$108	$114	$100	$96	$4

By eliminating these paths, the investor lowers the potential probability-adjusted payoff by:

$$= \text{PV} \ [(6/64 \times \$4.00) + (1/64 \times \$14.00)] = \text{PV} \ (\$0.59375)$$
$$= \$0.57$$

Thus, the premium of a regular put is $0.57 higher than the premium of a put with a $105 knock-out. Likewise, the price of a regular put minus the price of a $105 knock-out would equal the price of a $105 knock-in with the same strike and other parameters. Logic and arbitrage dictate that a knock-out plus a knock-in equals a normal put.

APPLICATIONS OF BARRIERS

The applications for barrier options are only limited by an investor's creativity. Here are a few common applications:

- Reduce the cost of put protection
- Enforce an outlook on volatility and direction
- Improve stop-loss protection
- Automate a trading strategy

Reduce the Cost of Put Protection

Consider this dilemma: An investor buys a stock at $40 that subsequently rises to $100. The investor believes the stock will go higher but is worried that the next earnings announcement due in 2 weeks may be disappointing. If it is, the stock will drop—perhaps significantly. However, if the earnings are good, the stock will probably rise by 5% or more.

The first possible solution would be for the investor to sell the stock and rebuy it if the earnings are good. The problems with this approach are that it creates a tax liability on the gain and the stock might rise significantly above the sale price before the investor can get back in.

The second possible solution would be to buy insurance in the form of a short-term listed $100 put option. This is fairly expensive because it is an ATM put. The expense of buying the put would be offset by the revenue from reselling it if the earnings were good and the price rose to $105. Of course, the put's sale price would be much lower than its purchase price if the stock started rising.

The third solution would be to buy an up-and-out put that was automatically canceled if the price reaches $105—the barrier. This option would be cheaper than the traditional put because it provides less protection. If the stock price rose to $106 and then fell to $70, the traditional put would provide protection, while the up-and-out would not. If the investor was convinced that if the price reached $105, insurance at $100 would no longer be necessary, this third alternative makes sense.

Enforce an Outlook on Volatility and Direction

Using the information found in the price tree depicted in Figure 16.4, suppose that, based on technical analysis, an investor thought a stock was going to take a temporary dip from $100 down to < $88.00 and then soar. One way to play this would be to buy an ATM put today and when the price bottoms, sell the put and buy an ATM call.

A smarter (reward per dollar at risk) way to play this outlook would be to buy:

- A down-and-in put with a strike at $100 and a knock-in at $88. This option would be much cheaper than a $100 put today—but would be worth the same $15 as the traditional $100 put if the stock was at $85 on expiration day
- A down-and-in call with a strike at $88 and a knock-in at $88. This option would be cheaper than buying an $88 call after the price declines to $85 but would be worth the same $12 if the stock rose back to $100 on expiration day.

As another possibility, suppose the price initially declines to $88, the investor has a put with $12 of intrinsic value that can be cashed out, and a call at $88 gets activated. The call has an unlimited upside.

If the price subsequently rises to $106, the investor has a call with $18 of intrinsic value. The investor's payoff would be the total price change over the path—not just the difference between the start and end value. The probability of this path being followed is 1 in 64, so the options together would be priced as shown in Figure 16.5.

FIGURE 16.5

Path Dependent Pricing

						$136.00
					$130.00	
				$124.00		$126.00
			$118.00		$120.00	
		$112.00		$114.00		$116.00
	$106.00		$108.00		$110.00	
$100.00		$102.00		$104.00		$106.00
	$96.00		$98.00		$100.00	
		$92.00		$94.00		$96.00
			$88.00		$90.00	
				$84.00		$86.00
					$80.00	
						$76.00

$$PV(\text{win} \times \text{prob}) = PV(\$30.00 \times 1/64) = PV(\$0.47) = \$0.45$$

If the path is followed and the $88 barrier is breached, $0.45 becomes $30—a multiple of 65 times original investment.

Improve Stop-Loss Protection

Another application of barrier options is to improve stop-loss protection. Many sophisticated investors use stop-losses to manage their risks. If they buy a stock at $100, they put a $95 stop-loss order in so that, if the stock moves down, they limit their loss to 5%. As the stock rises, the investors raise the prices of their stop-loss orders—keeping them at around 5% below the high. The problem with this approach is that, if prices spike down and then spike up because of a market hiccup, the stock is sold and then has to be repurchased at a higher price, as shown in Figure 16.6.

FIGURE 16.6
Impact of Stop Order

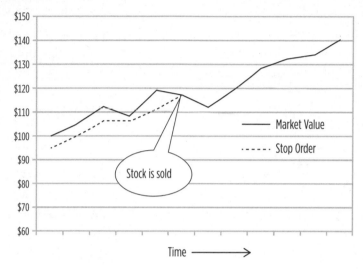

The alternative to a stop order is a series of knock-out and knock-in options. Initially, go long the stock with the following barrier option:

> $100 strike put with a $95 knock-in and a $105 knock-out

If the stock drops to $95, the knock-in option is activated and the investor can sell the stock at $100—losing only the option premium. However, if the $105 barrier is breached, the knock-out is activated and the option is canceled. Even though the option is canceled, breaching $105 activates the first of the dual triggers below the option and replaces the option that was canceled:

> $105 strike put with a dual barrier ($105 and then $100 knock-in) and a $110 knock-out

If the stock drops to $100, the second trigger for the above option is thrown and the investor can sell at $105. Or, if the $110 barrier is breached, a different second trigger is thrown and the above option is canceled. Even though the above option is canceled, breaching $110 is the first trigger to activating the below option, which replaces the one that was canceled:

> $110 strike put with a dual barrier ($110 and then $105 knock-in) and a $115 knock-out

By using a series of options with progressive knock-out and knock-in prices, the investor's level of price protection rises as the stock price rises. By using options instead of stop-loss orders, the investor doesn't automatically sell in a downturn. If the downturn is a short-lived spike, the investor lets the put expire and continues to own the rising asset.

Automate a Trading Strategy

Suppose a stock has established a trading range between $28 (support) and $34 (resistance). The stock is currently at $30. An investor could place the four option orders shown in Figure 16.8 and execute a classic support-resistance trading strategy.

FIGURE 16.7

Illustration of Trading Range

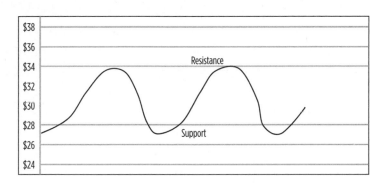

Up-and-in $35 call at $35 barrier

Up-and-in $34 put at $33 barrier with a knock-out at $35

Down-and-in $28 call at $29 barrier with a knock-out at $27

Down-and-in $27 put at $27 barrier

The logic for the four positions is as follows. As the stock reaches its:

- Support line, it should attract buyers and pop up—hence the $28 call—but if it breaks support, then the $28 call is canceled and the $27 put is activated
- Resistance line, it should attract sellers and drop down—hence the $34 put—but if it breaks resistance, the $34 put is canceled and the $35 call is activated

These steps simply automate what an investor who traded on technical analysis would do so the investor can manage more positions.

LOOKBACK OPTIONS

Another way barrier options can be combined is to make a lookback call. This is a call option where the strike price is reset to the lowest price the underlying trades at between the start date and the expiration date, as shown in Figure 16.8. Thus, if the stock is at $100 on the start date and then drops to $78.27 and then rises to $120 at expiration, the payoff equals:

> Max(0, expiration – lowest value at which underlying
> trades)

FIGURE 16.8

Path Dependent

						$163.21
					$150.42	
			$138.62			$138.62
		$127.76			$127.76	
	$117.74		$117.74			$117.74
$108.51		$108.51		$108.51		
$100.00		$100.00		$100.00		$100.00
	$92.16		$92.16		$92.16	
		$84.93		$84.93		$84.93
			$78.27		$78.27	
				$72.14		$72.14
					$66.48	
						$61.27

In the tree shown in Figure 16.8, the payoff would be $21.73, even though the initial price and final price are the same.

For a lookback put, the strike price would be the highest price along the path and the payoff is:

Max(0, highest value at which underlying trades –
    expiration)

Lookbacks:

- Are path dependent
- Are always at or in the money
- Can have a complete or a partial lookback period
- Are more expensive than traditional options
- Are really just a large collection of barriers that cancel and reset the strike as the price changes

The only way a lookback call can expire worthless is if the underlying trades at its lowest value right at expiration (highest value for a lookback put).

Pricing Lookback Options

To price a lookback option, trace each path from the starting value to the end value. Determine the payoff by subtracting the lowest value from the payoff value. Multiply each result by the path's probability. Sum the results for each path and PV the results. The calculation is illustrated in Figure 16.9.

FIGURE 16.9

Pricing Lookback Option

							Total Paths	Lookback Strike	Terminal Value	Number Paths	Prob. Path	Option Value
						$163.21	1	$100.00	$163.21	1	2.24%	$1.41
					$150.42			$100.00	$138.62	5	1.98%	$3.82
				$138.62		$138.62	6	$92.16	$138.62	1	1.98%	$0.92
			$127.76		$127.76			$100.00	$117.74	9	1.75%	$2.79
		$117.74		$117.74		$117.74	15	$92.16	$117.74	5	1.75%	$2.24
	$108.51		$108.51		$108.51			$84.93	$117.74	1	1.75%	$0.57
$100.00		$100.00		$100.00		$100.00	20	$92.16	$100.00	9	1.54%	$1.09
	$92.16		$92.16		$92.16			$84.93	$100.00	5	1.54%	$1.16
		$84.93		$84.93		$84.93	15	$78.27	$100.00	1	1.54%	$0.34
			$78.27		$78.27			$78.27	$84.93	5	1.37%	$0.45
				$72.14		$72.14	6	$72.14	$84.93	1	1.37%	$0.17
					$66.48			$66.48	$72.14	1	1.21%	$0.07
						$61.27	1				Sum	$15.04
											PV	$14.30

Modified Lookback Options

Another way barrier options can be combined is to make a modified lookback call. This is a call option where the strike price is the starting value, but the payoff is tied to the highest value the stock achieves along the path. Thus, once the option goes in the money, the value is never lost, as shown in Figure 16.10. The payoff is:

Modified lookback call options = Max(0, Max Value
    Along Path – Starting Value)
Modified lookback put options = Max(0, Starting Value –
    Min. Value Along Path)

FIGURE 16.10

Path Through Tree

						$163.21
					$150.42	
				$138.62		$138.62
			$127.76		$127.76	
		$117.74		$117.74		$117.74
	$108.51		$108.51		$108.51	
$100.00		$100.00		$100.00		$100.00
	$92.16		$92.16		$92.16	
		$84.93		$84.93		$84.93
			$78.27		$78.27	
				$72.14		$72.14
					$66.48	
						$61.27

Payoff for this path for call is $117.74 – $100.00 = $17.74.

These options are priced the same way that the regular lookbacks are priced—by tracing every path through the tree and de-

FIGURE 16.11

Pricing Modified Lookback Option

							Total Paths	Lookback Strike	Terminal Value	Highest Value	Number Paths	Prob. Path	Option Value
						$163.21	1		$163.21	$163.21	1	2.24%	$1.41
					$150.42			$100.00	$138.62	$150.42	1	1.98%	$1.00
				$138.62		$138.62	6	$100.00	$138.62	$138.62	5	1.98%	$3.82
			$127.76		$127.76		15	$100.00	$117.74	$138.62	1	1.75%	$0.67
		$117.74		$117.74		$117.74		$100.00	$117.74	$127.76	5	1.75%	$2.43
	$108.51		$108.51		$108.51			$100.00	$117.74	$117.74	9	1.75%	$2.79
$100.00		$100.00		$100.00		$100.00	20	$100.00	$100.00	$127.76	1	1.54%	$0.43
	$92.16		$92.16		$92.16			$100.00	$100.00	$117.74	5	1.54%	$1.37
		$84.93		$84.93		$84.93	15	$100.00	$100.00	$108.51	9	1.54%	$1.18
			$78.27		$78.27			$100.00	$84.93	$117.74	1	1.37%	$0.24
				$72.14		$72.14	6	$100.00	$84.93	$108.51	5	1.37%	$0.58
					$66.48			$100.00	$72.14	$108.51	1	1.21%	$0.10
						$61.27	1					Sum	$16.03
												PV	$15.24

termining its value and then multiplying that value by the volatility, as shown in Figure 16.11, for the example shown in Figure 16.10.

Chooser Options

A chooser option is an option that has a set strike price (usually the forward market value) and expiration date. What makes it an "exotic" is that, initially, it is not defined as a call or as a put. Instead, somewhere along the option's life—on the "choice date"—the investor decides whether the option will be a call or a put. Suppose a stock is selling at $200, expires in a year, and has a choice date in 6 months. Obviously, in 6 months, if the price of the stock is above $200, the investor will elect to make the option a call. If the price is below $200, the investor will elect to make the option a put. Once made, the choice decision is usually irrevocable.

A chooser is used in the same circumstances as straddles, such as takeovers, lawsuit results, significant new product releases, corporate restructurings, and management turnovers. In all these cases, the volatility is high—but direction is uncertain. To price a chooser, consider the following logical framework. If the choice date is:

The expiration date—When the choice date is the expiration date, the only way both options end up being worthless is if the stock is selling at exactly $200 when the options expire. If the price is above or below $200, the investor would choose to make the option a call or a put, respectively. Since the election would be made right at expiration, there is no time for the stock price to change enough for the in-the-money option to finish out of the money. In this case, the price of the chooser would have to be the price of an

ATM call *plus* the price of an ATM put. If the choice date and expiration date are the same, the option is always in or at the money. It's the equivalent of a straddle.

The start date—In this case, the price of the chooser would have to be the price of an ATM call *or* an ATM put, depending on the investor's choice. The choice component has no value; the price doesn't have time to move from $200.

Between the start and expiration dates—As the choice date moves from the expiration date and toward the start date, the probability of the choice option ending up out of the money after the investor decides call or put increases—and the price of the chooser declines.

As always, there is a trade-off between the option's price and the probability of the option having intrinsic value.

Dealers who create choosers price them one of two ways. They either price them by determining the cost of hedging the position or by modeling the option.

PRICING BY HEDGING

Suppose palladium is selling for $1,000 per ounce. The 1-year forward price is $1,050 and the 2-year forward price is $1,100. A trader wants to price and hedge a 2-year option with a 1-year choice date.

To hedge this chooser, the trader goes long a 2-year call at $1,100 and long a 1-year $1,050 put. In 1 year, if palladium is selling for:

More than $1,100—The investor will elect to make the chooser option a call. In this case, the trader's put expires.

The trader still has a call to offset the investor's call, so the trader is hedged.

Less than $1,100—The investor will elect to make the chooser option a put. The trader exercises the $1,050 put, borrows the palladium necessary to make delivery, and invests the $1,050 received, so it will become $1,100 in a year. When the dealer exercises the put, the dealer creates a short position in the metal, plus being long a call. Being "short the underlying" and being "long a call" is equal to owning a put, so the trader is again hedged. In 1 year's time, if:

- Palladium is above $1,100, the investor's put is worthless. The dealer uses the call option and its $1,100 cash to buy the palladium and return it to the party from whom it borrowed the metal a year earlier.
- Palladium is below $1,100, the investor will use the put to sell the dealer the palladium at $1,100. The dealer uses its $1,100 to pay the investor for the palladium and delivers the metal it receives from the investor to cover its short position.

The dealer will price the option at the cost of the two offsetting options plus a small margin.

PRICING VIA A MODEL

Look at the tree shown in Figure 16.12. Suppose the third step (shaded) is the choice date. If the price is one of the top two prices, the investor will elect to make the option a call. From the price of $127.76, the price can end up at four prices—three of which are in the money. From the price of $108.51, the price can end up at four prices—two of which are in the money. The payoffs, number of

FIGURE 16.12

Pricing a Chooser Contract

							Start	End	Value	Paths	Prob. Path	Value
						$163.21	$127.76	$163.21	$63.21	1	2.24%	$1.41
					$150.42		$127.76	$138.62	$38.62	3	1.54%	$1.78
				$138.62		$138.62	$127.76	$117.74	$17.74	3	1.55%	$0.82
			$127.76 (Call)		$127.76		$108.51	$138.62	$38.62	3	1.54%	$1.78
		$117.74		$117.74		$117.74	$108.51	$117.74	$17.74	9	1.55%	$2.47
	$108.51		$108.51		$108.51							
$100.00		$100.00 (■)		$100.00		$100.00						
	$92.16		$92.16		$92.16		$92.16	$84.93	$15.07	9	1.37%	$1.86
		$84.93		$84.93		$84.93	$92.16	$72.14	$27.86	3	1.21%	$1.01
			$78.27 (Put)		$78.27		$78.27	$84.93	$15.07	3	1.37%	$0.62
				$72.14		$72.14	$78.27	$72.14	$27.86	3	1.21%	$1.01
					$66.48		$78.27	$61.27	$38.73	1	1.07%	$0.41
						$61.27						
											Sum	$13.20
											PV	$12.54

paths, and probability for each path can be determined just like a barrier.

ASIAN OPTIONS

Asian options are options where the payoff is not tied to the MV at expiration. Instead, the payoff is tied to the average price at which the underlying trades at over a time horizon. For example, if the time frame was the entire life of the option, the underlying could follow the path shown in Figure 16.13.

FIGURE 16.13

Path Through the Tree

							$163.21
						$150.42	
					$138.62		$138.62
				$127.76		$127.76	
			$117.74		$117.74		$117.74
		$108.51		$108.51		$108.51	
$100.00		$100.00		$100.00		$100.00	
	$92.16		$92.16		$92.16		
		$84.93		$84.93		$84.93	
			$78.27		$78.27		
				$72.14		$72.14	
					$66.48		
						$61.27	

In that case, the payoff from an ATM Asian call would be:

$$(\$100.00 + \$108.51 + \$117.74 + \$127.76 + \$117.74 + \$108.51 + \$100.00) / 7 = \$111.47 - \$100 = \$11.47$$

Naturally, the period over which prices are averaged is determined by the terms of the option. Asian options make it impossible to significantly manipulate the profitability of an option by changing the MV of the underlying just before expiration.

Quantos

Quantos are a very popular form of exotic option that are marketed in two forms: fixed and floating. Fixed quantos allow investors to isolate risks in multi-risk positions. For example, suppose a US investor wants to buy a call option on a Canadian stock. The US investor is exposed to the:

- Price and volatility risk of the Canadian stock
- CAD/USD exchange rate

Ideally, the US investor wants the stock price to rise, volatility to increase, and the Canadian dollar to strengthen. However, if the US investor expected the Canadian dollar to weaken, the US investor would only want exposure to the stock's price and volatility risk; he or she will want to eliminate the FX risk.

A fixed quanto option allows the US investor to assume the price risk, but lock in the rate at which the Canadian dollars received from exercising/selling the option can be exchanged for US dollars. The rate that is locked in for this FX exchange is usually the implied forward FX rate. Thus, a fixed quanto is a combination of a:

- Traditional call option on the price of the Canadian stock
- Variable-size forward contract on the exchange rate. The forward FX contract has to have a variable size because the in-

vestor doesn't know how many Canadian dollars, if any, the investor will want to convert to US dollars when the option expires.

A floating quanto retains exposure to both price and FX risks, but is priced and paid in US dollars as a convenience to the US investor—thus relieving the US investor of the hassle and expense of having to do any actual FX conversions.

OPTIONS ON MULTIPLE ASSETS

An option on multiple assets is an option where the payoff is either the minimum or the maximum of two options on two different assets. There are four basic types:

- Call on max payoff = $Max[Max(MV_1 - K_1, MV_2 - K_2), 0]$
- Call on min payoff = $Max[Min(MV_1 - K_1, MV_2 - K_2), 0]$
- Put on max payoff = $Max[Max(K_1 - MV_1, K_2 - MV_2), 0]$
- Put on min payoff = $Max[Min(K_1 - MV_1, K_2 - MV_2), 0]$

These options add a correlation dimension to the usual dimensions of volatility and direction. As the correlation between the underlying instruments increases, the probability that one of the options will be in the money declines. These options have numerous useful business applications. Consider the following examples:

A utility in the Midwest builds a power plant that can burn either natural gas or oil. Naturally, it will burn whichever fuel is cheaper. The utility, like many utilities these days, sells a large percentage of its production forward at a fixed price to industrial companies and various local governments. Therefore, it can't just "pass along" any increase in fuel costs to its customers.

The utility can achieve its financial goals provided it can buy:

- Oil at $100 a barrel or less
- Natural gas at $90 per barrel equivalent or less

As long as it can obtain *either* fuel below these prices, it will achieve its financial objectives. If *both* prices are above the utility's limit, it will buy the cheaper one—but will need a hedge that lowers the cost of the cheaper fuel to the utility's limit price. Thus:

$$\text{Call on Min Payoff} = \text{Max}[\text{Min}(MV_1 - K_1, MV_2 - K_2), 0]$$

This call is cheaper than individual calls on both oil and gas because when both are in the money only the cheaper one is exercised, as shown in Figure 16.14.

FIGURE 16.14

Net Fuel Cost

Situation	Oil Price	Gas Price	Utility Buys	Min($MV_1 - K_1$, $MV_2 - K_2$)	Option Pays	Net Fuel Cost
1	$90	$70	Gas	–$20 (Gas)	$0	$70
2	$90	$100	Oil	–$10 (Oil)	$0	$90
3	$110	$85	Gas	–$5 (Gas)	$0	$85
4	$105	$120	Oil	$5 (Oil)	$5	$100
5	$120	$100	Gas	$10 (Gas)	$10	$90

As another example, suppose that gold is selling at $2,000 an ounce, and silver is at $50. The Central Bank of Brazil plans to sell some metals in 3 months and use the proceeds to buy reals in the global market in order to support the real's value. The bank can sell gold at $2,000 or higher or silver at $50 or higher (see Figure 16.15). Thus:

Put on Min Payoff = Max[Min(K_1 – MV_1, 40 ×
K_2 – MV_2), 0]

FIGURE 16.15

Resulting Net Price

Situation	Gold	Silver	Bank Sells	Min(K_1 – MV_1, K_2 – MV_2)	Option Pays	Net Price
1	$2,400	$51	Gold	–$400 Gold	$0	$2,400
2	$1,900	$53	Silver	–$120 Silver (40 × –$3)	$0	$53
3	$2,245	$48	Gold	–$45 Gold	$0	$2,245
4	$1,950	$40	Gold	+$50 Gold	$50	$2,000
5	$1,600	$48	Silver	+$200 Silver (40 × $2)	$2 per ounce	$50

Note the multiplier of 40 times the silver to balance out the dollar amount with the gold ($2,000 = $50 × 40).

Spread Options

The payoff of a spread option is tied to the difference between two values. They require the expenditure of less capital than individual multiple positions and the value again has a "correlation dimension." There are countless applications.

Yield curve plays—Banks profit from a steep yield curve. They borrow short term (average 1 year) via now accounts and short-term CDs at low rates and lend long term (average 5 years) at higher rates. If the yield curve has a positive slope, a bank might be able to borrow at 1% and lend at 5%—making a 4% spread. If the spread narrows, so does the bank's profit margin. The bank might want an option that pays the bank if the curve flattens and the bank's spread narrows.

Credit spreads—A Ba-rated company that was planning on borrowing money in 6 months would be exposed to the risk that the credit spread would widen. Of course, an investor expecting to invest in 6 months would be worried that the spread would narrow. He or she could use an option on the relevant credit spread (Ba vs. Treasuries). The borrower would buy an option that paid the investor if the spread widened out an option that paid if the spread narrowed.

Bid-ask spreads—Dealers are worried that bid-ask spreads in the markets will be too low to allow them to make an adequate profit from marking a market. Hedge funds and other active traders worry that the spreads will be too wide—reducing the profits from their trades and/or making some short-term strategies impossible to implement profitably. The dealers can buy an option that pays them if the spread narrows, and the investors should buy options that pay if the spread widens.

Combined long-short positions—An investor who thought that oil stocks would rise and airline stocks would fall could buy an option that pays off if the spread between the price of an oil index and an airline index widens. Another investor who believes the spread between the indices will narrow would be the seller.

FX rate spreads—A US company that was receiving money in one currency (for example, JPY) and paying in another currency (GBP) would worry that the spread between their values would change if the GBP strengthening against the USD while the JPY weakened. The US company would buy an option that paid when the spread widened. A US company that had the opposite currency flows would want to have an option that paid when the spread narrowed.

Commodity spreads—An oil refiner wants the spread between crude oil and finished products (gasoline, diesel, propane) to be as wide as possible. If the spread is too narrow, then the company won't make a profit refining crude. The consumers of the final products want the spread to be low; otherwise, their costs rise. A refiner might buy an option that pays if the spread is very narrow. Customers might buy an option that pays if the spread is too wide. In addition to oil refiners, spread options would also interest:

- Soybean processors who turn soybeans into soybean meal and soybean oil
- Sugarcane processors who turn sugarcane into sugar
- Shipping companies who burn bunker oil and charge container rates

The business applicability of spread options seems almost limitless.

BASKET OPTIONS

As the name implies, the price of a basket option is tied to the performance of a basket of stocks, bonds, FX rates, commodities, collectibles, or indicators. In addition to the items in the basket and their correlations, the option's value is also determined by the way the items are weighted: starting values, equal weighting, or customized weighting. Consider the following example that uses a basket of three stocks:

Initial prices: A = $20, B = $30, C = $40   Total = $90

Final prices: A = $40, B = $30, C = $20   Total = $100

If the basket is weighted by starting price:

Initial value [(1/90) × 20] + [(1/90) × 30] + [(1/90) × 40] = 1

Final value [(1/90) × 40] + [(1/90) × 30] + [(1/90) × 30] = 1.1111

Return (1.1111 − 1.0000) / 1.000 = 11.11%

If the basket is equally weighted, then the basket would contain $40 of each:

2.0000 shares of A (2.0000 × $20) = $40

1.3333 shares of B (1.3333 × $30) = $40

1.0000 shares of C (1.0000 × $40) = $40

Initial value = (2 × $20) + (1.3333 × $30) + (1 × $40) = $120

Final value = (2 × $40) + (1.3333 × $30) + (1 × $30) = $150

Return = ($150 − $120) / $120 = 25.00%

If the basket is custom-weighted and:

A is weighted 50%

B is weighted 30%

C is weighted 20%

Initial value = (.5 × $20) + (.3 × $30) + (.2 × $40) = $27

Final value = (.5 × $40) + (.3 × $30) + (.2 × $30) = $35

Return ($35 − $27) / $27 = 29.63%

Thus, the payoff of this option depends to a great extent on how the basket is weighted—the small print matters.

CAPPED OPTIONS

A capped option is an option where the profit is limited or "capped." By capping the profit for the long, the loss is capped for the short. Because the loss is capped for the short, the short can charge a lower premium for a capped option than a regular option. For example, suppose the gain on a $200 call option on IBM is capped at $25. The payoff would be as shown in Figure 16.16.

FIGURE 16.16
Payoff for Capped Options

Price of IBM at Expiration	Payoff for Capped Option
$200 or Below	$0
$205	$5
$210	$10
$215	$15
$220	$20
$225 or Above	$25

Economically, a capped option is the equivalent of an option spread. For the option depicted in Figure 16.16, the equivalent position is a bull call spread—long a $200 call and short a $225 call.

EXECUTIVE STOCK OPTIONS

Executive stock options are granted to senior personnel for several reasons:

- To align the executives' interests with the shareholders' interests
- To place "golden hand cuffs" on talented people, making it harder for competitors to recruit them

Executive stock options almost always come with a vesting schedule. This is the schedule by which the title to the options transfers from the company to the executive. A 5-year vesting schedule is typical.

The value of an executive option is dependent upon how long it is until the option vests and the frequency of executive turnover. For example, if the company loses 10% of its executives per year and the options vest in 5 years, there is only a 50% chance the executive will be around long enough for the options to vest. If there is only a 50% chance the options will vest, that reduces the probability that the option will ever be in the money by 50%. Thus, if a plain vanilla option is worth $30, this option is worth $15. As time passes and the vesting date approaches, the value gap between the value of the executive and the plain option declines, as shown in Figure 16.17.

FIGURE 16.17

Pricing of Executive Options

Time to Vesting	Value Exec Option	Value Reg Option
5 years	$15	$30
4 years	$18	$30
3 years	$21	$30
2 years	$24	$30
1 year	$27	$30
Vested	$30	$30

STEP-UP AND STEP-DOWN OPTIONS

A step-up (or step-down) option is one where the strike price changes either on a predetermined schedule or as tied to an index. Again, they are collections of barrier options. A common application of these options is as part of executive compensation. The strike price of executive options is often raised each year by the company's cost of capital. After all, if all a company earns is a return equal to its cost of capital, then it is just treading water and management should not be rewarded. Only returns in excess of the cost of capital benefit shareholders, so management must either figure out how to raise returns or to lower the cost of capital.

TRUE EXOTICS OPTIONS

A true exotic option is one where no pricing model exists. You can't just enter the strike and volatility into Bloomberg or another investor platform and, presto, "get the theoretical value." Each situation is different and demands a customized solution. Some examples will illustrate the concept.

Farmers are very dependent on the weather. Consider a corn farmer in Pennsylvania. The growing season in the state is 150 days, and farmers need 120 of those 150 days to be between 75 and 95 degrees in order to maximize their yield. Suppose a farmer wanted to hedge the temperature risk and that the following are true:

- Every day beyond 120 that the temperature disappointed, the cost to the farmer is $10,000 in either reduced yield or higher costs.
- The mean temperature was 85 degrees with a 5-degree standard deviation.
- The risk-free rate was 3%.
- It is 150 days before the end of the growing season.

What should temperature protection cost? The farmer needs to be paid $10,000 for each day above 30 days that the temperature is outside the growing range. Since the mean is 85 degrees with a 5-degree standard deviation, the farmer needs to be paid if the temperature is more than 2 standard deviations (high or low) from the mean. The chance of a result more than 2 standard deviations from the mean is 4%. Thus, the chance that the farmer will need a payoff is also 4%. A 4% chance of paying $10,000 is worth $400. Thus, the price of protection should be $400 a day—present valued. Technically, the formula is:

PV[(# Days Temp in Growing Season − 30) × $400]
= (120 × $400) / (1 + (.03 × 75/360))
= $47,702

FORWARDS WHERE THE
UNDERLYING CAN'T BE STORED

Forward contracts are also entered into on underlying instruments that can't be stored, such as wind, rain, temperature, snowfall, hurricane damage, and the like. All that is needed is two parties—one that benefits from an increase in the underlying and another that benefits from a decrease. For example:

- Airlines suffer significant losses when the wind exceeds its historic norms.
- Wind farms suffer when the wind is below historic norms.

An airline and wind farm could enter into a contract where the airline would pay the wind farm if wind levels were historically low and the wind farm would pay the airline if wind levels were historically high. This would allow both the airline and the wind farm to hedge this risk and smooth out their cash flows and earnings. Either party could also be replaced with a speculator looking for a risk that had no correlation with the stock market or bond market.

INDEX

Page numbers in **bold** indicate tables; those in *italics* indicate figures.

Stuart Veale is the president and founder of the Investment Performance Institute Inc., a firm that specializes in providing advanced-level practical capital markets training and consulting services to the financial services industry. Previously he was a senior vice president of portfolio strategy and design for the national sales group at Prudential Securities Inc. and senior vice president of advanced training at PaineWebber Inc.

Over the last 30 years, Mr. Veale has trained more than 6,000 capital markets professionals on portfolio design, trading strategies, risk analysis, derivative pricing and strategies, fixed income portfolio management, equity pricing and analysis, CFA I and II Prep, and numerous other securities-related topics. He has published six books: *The Handbook of the U.S. Capital Markets* (Harper Business), *Bond Yield Analysis* (New York Institute of Finance), *Tapping the Small Business Market* (New York Institute of Finance), *Essential Investment Math* (International Financial Press), *Essential Asset Allocation* (International Financial Press), and *Stocks, Bonds, Options, Futures* (Prentice Hall Press). He has also published numerous financial articles in magazines such as *Registered Representative*, *Cash Flow Magazine*, and *Medical Economics*.